On Being Maya
and Getting By

IMS STUDIES ON CULTURE AND SOCIETY SERIES

On Being Maya and Getting By

Heritage Politics and Community
Development in Yucatán

SARAH R. TAYLOR

UNIVERSITY PRESS OF COLORADO
Boulder

© 2018 by University Press of Colorado

Published by University Press of Colorado
245 Century Circle, Suite 202
Louisville, Colorado 80027

The University Press of Colorado is a proud member of
the Association of American University Presses.

 The University Press of Colorado is a proud member of
the Association of University Presses.

The University Press of Colorado is a cooperative publishing enterprise supported, in part, by Adams State University, Colorado State University, Fort Lewis College, Metropolitan State University of Denver, Regis University, University of Colorado, University of Northern Colorado, Utah State University, and Western State Colorado University.

∞ This paper meets the requirements of the ANSI/NISO Z39.48-1992 (Permanence of Paper).

ISBN: 978-1-60732-771-4 (cloth)
ISBN: 978-1-60732-857-5 (paperback)
ISBN: 978-1-60732-772-1 (ebook)
DOI: https://doi.org/10.5876/9781607327721

Library of Congress Cataloging-in-Publication Data

Names: Taylor, Sarah R., author.
Title: On being Maya and getting by : heritage politics and community development in Yucatán / Sarah R. Taylor.
Description: Boulder : University Press of Colorado, [2018] | Includes bibliographical references and index.
Identifiers: LCCN 2018012512| ISBN 9781607327714 (cloth) | ISBN 9781607328575 (pbk) | ISBN 9781607327721 (ebook)
Subjects: LCSH: Heritage tourism—Mexico—Ekbalam. | Ekbalam Site (Mexico) | Yucatán (Mexico : State)—Antiquities. | Mayas—Antiquities.
Classification: LCC G155.M6 T39 2018 | DDC 338.4/7917265—dc23
LC record available at https://lccn.loc.gov/2018012512

Portions of chapter 6 appeared in "Maya Cosmopolitans: Engaging Tactics and Strategies in the Performance of Tourism," *Identities* 21, no. 2 (2014): 219–32, DOI: 10.1080/1070289X.2013.878250. Portions of chapter 7 appeared in "Issues in Measuring Success in Community-Based Indigenous Tourism: Elites, Kin Groups, Social Capital, Gender Dynamics, and Income Flows," *Journal of Sustainable Tourism* 25, no. 3 (2017): 433–49, DOI: 10.1080/09669582.2016.1217871.

Cover photograph by Sarah R. Taylor, 2007.

For Lupe, of course.

Contents

Figures

Foreword

It is easy for tourists and even anthropologists to romanticize the Yucatán peninsula. From the beautiful tropical beaches on the coastline to the magnificent Maya archaeological sites that are found throughout the region and interspersed by small Maya villages and cities with Spanish Colonial architecture. Sarah R. Taylor's monograph, *On Being Maya and Getting By: Heritage Politics and Community Development in Yucatán*, captures this romanticism of the Yucatán and then expertly complicates it, as any excellent ethnographic work should.

Anyone marginally familiar with the Yucatán will recognize there is something for every kind of tourist, and for those tourists who like to do a bit of everything—from exploring contemporary and historical Maya culture to sampling regional delicacies like *cochinita pipil*, suckling pig cooked in an earthen pit, and *sikil p'ak*, a dish made of ground pumpkin seeds. From the Cancún international airport, it is minutes to beach resorts and luxury hotels. An easy hour-and-a-half drive south through the Maya Riviera is Tulum, a Maya archaeological site that survived into the Spanish colonial invasion. Turning inland, it's another one and a half hours to Valladolid, which, like the larger city Mérida and the smaller, Izamal, offers tourists cosmopolitan urban experiences and Spanish colonial history and architecture. Well-known Maya archaeological sites like Chichén Itzá and Uxmal, roughly two hours and four hours by car from Cancún, respectively, draw thousands of tourists, but the peninsula has dozens of smaller accessible sites and Maya villages, nestled among henequin plantations, and scrubby thorny forests, that contrast starkly with the capital cities of the region.

One of the region's especially distinctive qualities, outside of Cancún and the hyper-developed Maya Riviera that includes Cozumel and Playa de Carmen, is that it largely does not feel overridden with tourism. Certainly Chichén Itzá gets its fair share of the nearly two million who visit the peninsula, but less toured places can be found in abundance and make for experiences that do not seem all that touristy. One such place is Ek'Balam, the location of this wonderful ethnography.

As I am a Guatemalanist anthropologist who has studied Maya handicraft vendors and artisans in tourism marketplaces for thirty years, my connections to the Yucatán are a mix of personal engagements, touristic, academic, and social. So it is as an interloper that I offer my thoughts here. My first trip to this region was in 1986. I had vague goals of seeing authentic Maya architectural sites and a very specific goal of avoiding tourist traps like Cancún, thinking myself a traveler, rather than a tourist. The Maya Riviera had not yet been developed into a tourism resort zone and it was still possible to sleep for free on the beach below Tulum. Ek'Balam, the contemporary village or the archaeological site, was not yet integrated into the tourism circuit, but there were more than enough archaeological sites to explore and little Maya villages to visit to give the impression of being off the beaten path. In hindsight, I know I was not.

It is important to remember, whether one is a tourist or an anthropologist, that tourism in the Yucatán has been carefully cultivated by the Mexican government and local residents for decades. Tourism's influence, deep and far-reaching, has been studied by cultural anthropologists for decades now. Taylor's book adds to the tourism scholarship of this region that has included Alice Littlefield's study of the hammock industry in the 1970s, Quetzil Castañeda's research on Maya archeological sites and Maya artisans from the 1980s to the present, and M. Bianet Castellanos's investigation of Maya migrant laborers to Cancún since the 1990s. Such scholarship offers a window into Maya worldviews and socioeconomic ecologies of development.

In 2013, when I finally returned to visit the Yucatán, it was in part to visit Taylor at Ek'Balam. My sensibilities had been reshaped by long-term research in Guatemala, where political and social violence, if not immediately present, is always percolating under the surface. Arriving in Valladolid at dusk, my spouse and I decided it was too dangerous to drive the final half hour to Ek'Balam. Instead, we called Taylor and asked the family to forgive us for not coming to dinner. We were not given the option of skipping dinner and soon found ourselves back in the rental car, navigating dark, curving roads; getting lost; and eventually arriving to the best pork spare-ribs we have ever eaten. Sitting around the kitchen hearth with Taylor and our hosts, we were reminded, for the first of many times, that Yucatán is not Guatemala; that it is not even Mexico when it comes to safety and violence. At the same time, I was struck by how much my hosts participated in the same kinds of international tourism that the Guatemalan Mayas do, tempered by their distinctive cultural and linguistic perspectives. Here, too, are people whose lives are so entangled in tourism that there is no real distinction between life inside and outside of it. Taylor helps us see this in this book without reifying touristic tropes or simplifying the people of Ek'Balam.

The residents of Ek'Balam are part of tourism, mixed up in it, like all Mayas living in this region of Mesoamerica. Some residents do participate in construction projects in resorts on the Maya Riviera coastline, just as others work as restaurant waiters and hotel staff. Some work as professional, government-authorized guides at the neighboring archaeological site, also known as Ek'Balam. Women in the village still make hammocks for local and touristic consumption, while men carefully tend their *milpas* to ensure the best possible maize harvest. In these endeavors, they are like many other Mayas living in the Yucatán. What stands out in Taylor's work, in comparison to other ethnographies of Maya tourism, including my own of Antigua Guatemala, is that Taylor explores the inner workings of a community that is experimenting with how to participate in tourism. Drawing on more than a decade of experience, she shares how Ek'Balam residents actively seek positive economic development of their community according to their needs, utilizing government and non-governmental resources that inspire rethinking of what sustainable development and community-based development mean, all the while adhering to their own values. This is by no means a simple task. They are caught within the complex power dynamics of local community politics, where their cultural values, economic strategies, and social and kin and family relations are debated and negotiated, as are their strategies for contending with the far more powerful Mexican state and international tourism industry.

Taylor takes the reader into Ek'Balam households to show how families navigate touristic constructions of Maya identity in relation to their own senses of self. This leads to contradictions that result in Maya in this small town being both sophisticated cosmopolitans and farmer-artisans at the same time. Taylor skillfully demonstrates how their critical, hopeful, and skeptical engagement with foreign and Mexican tourists and tourism industries can lead to entrepreneurial challenges and successes without the compromise of their core cultural values.

Walter Little
Professor of Anthropology
University at Albany, SUNY

Acknowledgments

This ethnography, like all of those that have come before it, is only possible because of the support and contributions I received from many people at home and in the field. I would like to acknowledge and thank them here. The greatest debt is, of course, owed to the residents of Ek'Balam. Their patience and generosity allowed me to begin this research and the friendship and good humor of many families and individuals enabled me to complete it. In particular, I am grateful to doña Guadalupe Balam Canche and don Andres Ay Tuz, who have been my friends and hosts since the day I first arrived in Ek'Balam. Their family kept me fed, safe, and healthy, and has vouched for the character of their *gringa* more than once. Most of my early knowledge of Yucatec Maya was gained in their household through patient repetition and teasing. Their children— Mauricio, Beatrice, Angel, Alberto, Jose, and Maria de la Cruz—never tired of my questions about this word or that and made marvelous teachers. Their son-in-law, Teofilo, is always ready and willing to tell stories and answer questions. I would also like to thank don Mario Tuz May, don Guteberto Mena Tuz, and don Federico Chan Tuz for their enormous contributions to this research.

They graciously allowed me to accompany them into the *milpa* and forest any time I asked, and somehow never tire of recounting the old stories and explaining the most mundane activities. They also shared with me the history of the community-based tourism project and the successes and challenges it has had along the way. Their patience when asked to repeat themselves and their gentle teasing about some of my more ridiculous questions make them the best collaborators an ethnographer could imagine. Lee Christie also deserves thanks for her friendship and provision of creature comforts during many hot summers.

A number of mentors influenced and supported me through this research process. Walter E. Little, Robert Jarvenpa, Marilyn Masson, and Ronald Loewe all read the earliest versions of this book and each of them has influenced it in important ways. Jarvenpa taught me about the potentials of a political ecological approach and introduced the concept of an ecosystem to my research. Masson patiently shared her archaeological expertise of Yucatán. Loewe instilled the importance of reading Mexican ethnography and incorporating it into my research. Finally, Little modeled for me the commitment that long-term longitudinal ethnographic research entails and greatly influenced my understanding of Mesoamerican scholarship. I have the good fortune of conducting fieldwork in a region with a rich history of ethnography. Quetzil Castañeda, Ellen Kintz, Lisa Breglia, Alicia ReCruz, Francisco Fernández Repetto, Gabriela Vargas-Cetina, Steffan Igor Ayora Diaz, and Grace Bascopé all played a role in enriching my knowledge of life in Yucatán. Specifically, I owe a debt of gratitude to Alejandro Cabrera Valenzuela for sharing his deep knowledge of Ek'Balam and the surrounding communities. He is an excellent collaborator and a good friend. A number of archaeologists in Yucatán were patient with me as I learned about the pre-Colombian history of the area and about how local communities engage their archaeological heritage. Marilyn Masson, Jennifer Mathews, Bradley Russell, and Caroline Antonelli each helped me with this. Mesoamerica more broadly has a long ethnographic history, and Jayne Howell and Tim Wallace both influenced my knowledge of this history and its incorporation into my writing.

It may seem excessive to include undergraduate mentors in these acknowledgments; however, there are two individuals in particular at California State University, Chico who are in many ways responsible for this product. Charlotte Ekland introduced me to Yucatán, and William Loker encouraged me to spend a summer conducting independent fieldwork there. I am grateful to both of them for getting me started on this path.

A number of organizations supported this research over the years. The California State University, Chico Undergraduate Research and Creativity Award funded the 2004 fieldwork, and a grant from the American Philosophical Society's Lewis and Clark Fund supported a number of subsequent field seasons.

Final research and write-up were supported by the DeCormier Research Award from the Institute for Mesoamerican Studies and the Christine E. Bose and Edna Acosta-Belen IFW Feminist Research Award. The University at Albany, SUNY supported my research and writing through graduate assistantships. During my years there, I benefitted from many conversations with faculty and students and made some wonderful friends. Prominent among them are Heidi Nicholls and Christine Vassallo-Oby, for whom I am so grateful. Wichita State University supported me in the form of graduate research assistants during the revision stages. Lisa Lonning and Amanda Assaf were incredibly resourceful and helpful as I worked to revise this manuscript, and Juan R. Argueta Jr. did wonderful work on some of the maps included here. California State University, Dominguez Hills provided resources for indexing during the final stages of publication, and my colleagues in the Department of Anthropology at CSUDH contributed a great deal of enthusiasm.

The editorial team at University Press of Colorado has been a great support. Specifically, Jessica d'Arbonne who started the process and Laura Furney who is seeing it completed. Five anonymous reviewers read drafts and revisions and their feedback helped me write a much better book.

This process has been supported by numerous individuals in my personal life as well. I am indebted to my parents, Clark and Paula Taylor, who have always supported my goals, and to Bruce and Leslie Steidl and our Feather Falls family for teaching me to be curious and to believe in others and in myself. I want to acknowledge my mother-in-law, Joy Tash, and my friends the Kirkland family for being an endless fountain of encouragement during some of the challenges along the way. Finally, I would like to thank the people who are truly the foundation of this work: my husband, Sloan Tash, and our daughter, Clara Lux. Sloan has supported this endeavor emotionally, financially, and physically by both agreeing to brave winters in Albany, New York, and bearing the intense heat of Yucatán in July. I am amazed by his generosity, patience, and ability to find humor in all situations. I am also grateful to him for logistical support, including maintaining our household for months at a time while I am in the field and never, ever asking me not to go.

On Being Maya and Getting By

A Tale of Two Ek'Balams

Indigenous populations throughout Mexico have been the focus of state-led development for many years. With the development of tourism on the coast of the Mexican state of Quintana Roo in the 1970s, tourism became a vital tool for economic development projects. At the same time, the country was preparing for massive changes to the *ejidal* system—a communally based land tenure system dating back to the post-Revolutionary period of the 1920s and 1930s. By the mid-1990s, sweeping neo-liberal reforms to land policy throughout the country had fundamentally altered the land tenure system. The federal government was intent on modernizing the country's rural, peasant, and largely indigenous population. Trends in international development that favored a community-based approach to combat the numerous failings the top-down approach had yielded in previous decades were primary influences on this development process. These contemporaneous shifts in economic development, land tenure, and indigenous farming played out in a variety of ways in different parts of the country.

In the midst of these changes, the history of one village in the state of Yucatán took a unique turn when an important archaeological zone opened to the public

DOI: 10.5876/9781607327721.c000

just 300 meters from the town center. This book is about these two Ek'Balams: one is a notable archaeological site and the other is a community living in the shadow of this ancient urban center. In 1994, the archaeological zone of Ek'Balam became a destination, bringing tourists to the municipality for the first time. In 1996, the *ejido* entered into the land privatization process through a new government initiative. In 2001, the village became the site of a community-based tourism (CBT) development project funded by the Mexican government.

The site of Ek'Balam, or Black Jaguar in Yucatec Maya (Barrera Vázquez 1980), is one of forty-six archaeological zones in the region open for exploration by the 10 million tourists who travel in Yucatán and Quintana Roo each year (SEDETUR 2013; SEFOTUR 2014). The Mexican state of Quintana Roo, home of Cancún and the Maya Riviera, receives about one-third of all foreign tourist expenditures in Mexico, and since 1970, this state has had a higher rate of growth than any other part of Mexico (SECTUR 2014; Clancy 2001b). Cancún is the tourist emporium located on the northeast tip of the Yucatán Peninsula. Since its creation in the 1970s, it has become a destination famed for its white beaches, turquoise sea, and 280-kilometer coral reef. For guests it offers "good and predictable hotels, an exotic ambiance of margaritas and mariachis, lush tropical forests, and Maya ruins" (Pi-Sunyer, Thomas, and Daltabuit 2001, 122). More than 3 million visitors enter the Yucatán Peninsula region through the Cancún International Airport annually, 60 percent of whom are North Americans (SECTUR 2015). The final destination of the majority is the Maya Riviera, which refers to the Cancún-Tulum corridor stretching approximately 130 km from the northern tip of the peninsula south to the community of Tulum.

While the success of this destination is undeniable, there are costs associated with large-scale tourism development as well. Quintana Roo is home to some of the country's poorest and most malnourished citizens. In comparison to Mexico's national averages, this state has higher rates of infant mortality and divorce and a lower life expectancy (Juárez 2002; Arroyo et al. 2013). Development of Cancun and the Maya Riviera began as a government economic policy favoring international and national economic investment in the hotel industry. During this process, the Mexican state took on the new role of initiating and planning tourism development (Clancy 2001b). From the conception of the idea to the receipt of $21.5 million in funding from the Inter-American Development Bank (IDB) in 1971, the "Cancun Project" was orchestrated by the government through newly formed and empowered agencies such as FONATUR—the Fondo Nacional de Fomento al Turismo (National Tourism Development Fund) (Clancy 2001b, 133). To complete the Hotel Zone efficiently and quickly, cheap labor was necessary. The developers targeted the Maya population in the Yucatán Peninsula to satisfy this need. For the Maya, Cancún was an alternative to traditional milpa, or corn, production, which is uncertain and labor-intensive.

The development of Cancún added migration and wage labor to their economic possibilities. Peasants could now migrate to Cancún when the fields were resting and return to the community when they were needed for agricultural work. Mainly unskilled peasant Maya were recruited for the construction work. This also became an alternative for the young Maya, looking for an alternative to the periodic hardships of milpa production (Re Cruz 2003). This government-planned and internationally funded destination marked a shift in the way Mexico conducted and managed tourism.

Across the Yucatán Peninsula, state governments as well as agents of the federal government have embraced the ancient Maya heritage as their most important—and profitable—characteristic. More important, the state has identified the indigenous past as the tangible remnants of it as national patrimony. The country had long been the object of the touristic imagination, particularly for North Americans (Berger and Wood 2010); however, with the creation of FONATUR, the Mexican government established its first foray into the governance of tourism (Castañeda and Burtner 2010; Cheong and Miller 2000; Bramwell and Lane 2011; Dinica 2009). In some ways, this was an obvious extension of the existing role of the federal government in the promotion and management of heritage (Berger 2006; Muñoz-Fernández 2015). Since 1939, the Instituto Nacional de Antropología e Historia (National Institute of Anthropology and History, INAH) has governed the nation's patrimony in the form of archaeological zones.

The tourism industry effectively reinforces ethnic difference by using it as a primary marker of destinations throughout Latin America (Anderson 2013; Babb 2010; Baud and Ypeij 2009); however, Mexico's focus on the presentation of ancient indigenous peoples through archaeological exploration is a marked difference (Bueno 2010; Velasco 2016; Clark and Anderson 2015). New emphases on multiculturalism and neo-liberal development models in state and federal promotions of tourism in Mexico and the Yucatán Peninsula in particular complicate the view of Maya identity (Loewe 2009), with some viewing it as a colonialist construct (Castañeda 2004; Hervik 1998; Restall 1999) and others as a continuation of cultural traits from the pre-Columbian period. The promotion of tourism at archaeological sites brings into question issues such as politics of patrimony and the management of ruins, as well as the present-day negotiations surrounding land rights in archaeological zones and the internal and external forces involved (Breglia 2006). It is at this intersection of heritage, tourism, and identity that the archaeological zones for which the Mexican state of Yucatán is so well-known are positioned (Castañeda 1996, 2003; Walker 2009).

Tourism has left its mark on the region in both cultural and physical ways. A major tourist corridor cuts across the peninsula, connecting Mérida, the state capital of Yucatán, with the resorts of Cancún and the Maya Riviera (figure 0.1). These two cities represent different types of tourism experiences and provide

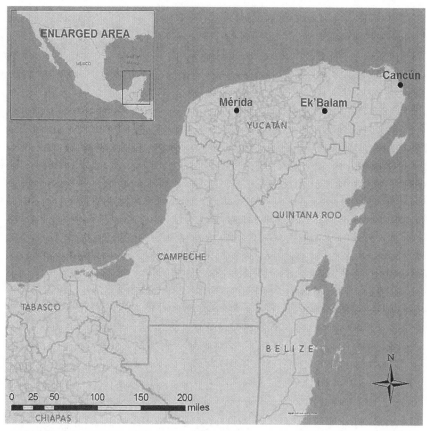

FIGURE 0.1. *Main tourist corridor through Yucatán*

vastly different offerings. On one side is a culturally vibrant colonial city and on the other are the white sand beaches of the Maya Riviera. These types of tourist destinations are the two ends of a typology of tourism, including mass or charter tourism, cultural tourism, and alternative tourism (Smith 1989). We can think of the typology of tourism as a spectrum. If alternative "off the beaten path" tourism is at one end, I propose that mass, or charter, tourism is on the other end. By identifying these two types of tourism and positioning them as opposites, we have just created a spectrum, or a continuum, of tourism. In addition, we have created tourism border zones to be traversed by hosts and guests alike (Bruner 2005).

Small villages, cities, archaeological zones, haciendas, forests, and the million Yucatec Maya who live on the peninsula (INEGI 2010) dot the length of this tourism continuum. In the 1930s, anthropologists descended on Yucatán and Mesoamerica more broadly, turning the region into a veritable ethnographic laboratory. Throughout Mesoamerica, anthropologists were concerned

FIGURE 0.2. *Castillo at Chichén Itzá (left) and Acropolis at Ek'Balam (right)*

with understanding the way indigenous people organized themselves socially into communities and how these "little communities" were key to gaining an understanding of indigenous, peasant culture. One of the lasting concepts that emerged from this period was the folk-urban continuum, as proposed by Robert Redfield (1941). Ethnographers subsequently adopted this model as a framework for understanding peasant communities throughout Latin America and even elsewhere in the world. They presumed that anyone who fit the description of "peasant" was at some stage of their journey from folk to urban. Anthropologists discarded this conceptual framework long ago, but the concept of the continuum serving as a gauge for a place and a person's rurality is alive and well in promotions of cultural, archaeological, and eco-tourism. Located in the literal and figurative middle of this continuum are the two Ek'Balams.

The archaeological zone of Ek'Balam is home to some of the most impressive pre-Columbian stuccoes found in the Maya World, and their excavation and subsequent opening of the site to visitors was a welcome addition to INAH's holdings. This is a Terminal Classic site that reached its height between AD 700 and 1100 (Bey et al. 1998; Sharer and Traxler 2006). One of the most important attractions at Ek'Balam today is the Acropolis. This structure is one of the largest monuments in the Northern Maya Lowland region (Vargas de la Peña, Borges, and García-Gallo 1998). More important, it is open for climbing and exploration. When the famous Castillo at Chichén Itzá closed in 2005, Ek'Balam's Acropolis became one of the two remaining pyramids for visitors to climb within day-trip range of both Mérida and Cancún (figure 0.2).

The Castillo at Chichén Itzá—a four-sided flattop pyramid—is perhaps the most widely recognizable icon of the Yucatán Peninsula. An average of 5,000 tourists visit this site daily, with the majority coming around the spring and fall equinoxes to bear witness to the shadow serpent descending the Castillo (UNESCO 2015). I visited Chichén Itzá as an exchange student and, similar to many of my fellow travelers, lesser-known destinations deemed to be off the beaten path piqued my interest. The growing popularity of Ek'Balam and its reputation among travelers as the alternative to Chichén Itzá are what attracted me to the area in 2003.

Travel to Ek'Balam is safe and easy, a characteristic of the region that adds to its allure for tourists. A comfortable two-hour bus ride takes visitors from their hotel in Mérida or Cancún to the colonial city of Valladolid. There they exit the bus station and are greeted immediately by taxi drivers who will chauffer them to Ek'Balam and bring them back about two hours later for around US$30 (560 Mexican pesos). This leaves them plenty of time to explore the archaeological site, climb the monuments, and purchase a few souvenirs. The drive to and from the archaeological site is pleasant and comfortable. A main highway heads north from Valladolid and passes through the town of Temozón, providing a glimpse of daily life. Ten kilometers north of Temozón a highway turns east and leads directly to the archaeological zone.

Adjacent to this ancient site is the modern-day village of Ek'Balam. This village of around 350 residents has experienced numerous changes since the initial excavation of the archaeological zone. Visitors arrive daily at the intersection of the main road into the archaeological zone and the smaller road that, according to barely visible hand-painted signs, leads to the Maya village of Ek'Balam. Not surprisingly, most choose to continue into the archaeological site on the road more traveled. For most, the narrow road full of potholes that reveal the white earth beneath the pavement does not look like the correct choice. Before its completion in 2003, the road to the ruins took a much different route (figure 0.3). The old road to the archaeological zone leads through the small village of Ek'Balam, past thatch houses, playing children, and roaming poultry before arriving at the ruins. Until the completion of the new road, the entrance to the archaeological zone was located just outside the village of Ek'Balam, approximately 300 meters from the zone's ceremonial center. The village of Ek'Balam has experienced numerous changes since the initial excavation of the archaeological zone. With the completion of the new road, travelers can easily bypass this scenery and get straight to the archaeological zone they came to see.

In 2003, I arrived at this intersection and opted to turn off the brand-new highway and into the village of Ek'Balam. After this initial visit to the archaeological zone and village of Ek'Balam, I became very interested in how this small community was engaging with such a major change to its daily life. While residents have always had ties to the regional economy, the opening of the archaeological zone represented their first extended local engagement with the tourism industry. A major agent of change in Ek'Balam is a community-based tourism (CBT) project that, until the completion of the new road in 2003, was located just outside the entrance to the site (figure 0.4). The CBT project is a hotel and cultural center called U Najil Ek'Balam, which means House of the Black Jaguar in Yucatec Maya.

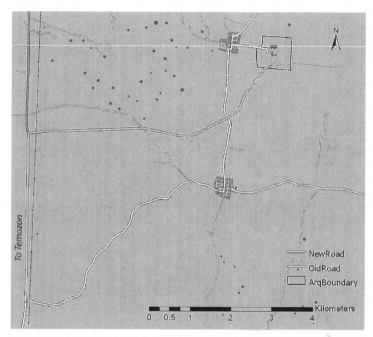

FIGURE 0.3. *Location of initial entrance to archaeological zone*

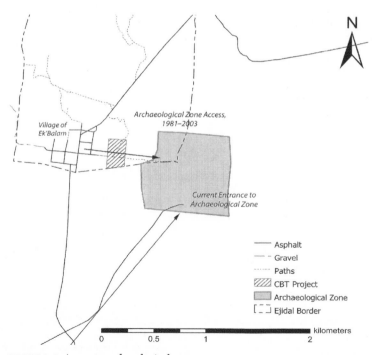

FIGURE 0.4. *Access to archaeological zone*

Residents were never isolated from tourism and tourists; however, managing a hotel down the street from one's house is categorically different from working on a construction crew building a hotel in Cancún, which was one of residents' main engagements with the region's tourism industry. This was the main topic of conversation with the individuals I met on that trip, and I decided that I wanted to know more about exactly how people were handling this change. Six months later I returned to embark on the research that would eventually answer these questions. Ek'Balam provides a context for understanding the many factors at work in development initiatives, kinship and land use, and the tourism encounter. The results of this analysis are a rich description of how one group of people is actively negotiating with tourism and development.

The Arrival of Tourism

In Mexico as in many countries, archaeological remains are the property of the nation and a source of patrimony (Vázquez Léon 2003). In Mexico particularly, this patrimony has been an important foundation for the creation and promotion of a national identity (García Canclini 1999). As part of the *indigenismo* movement, the pre-Colombian past in Mexico became an important key to promoting Mexico and Mexicans as hybrids of an indigenous past and a cosmopolitan future (García Canclini 1990; Saldívar 2011). The remnants of the past became the heritage of the nation (Breglia 2006; Castañeda 1996), which encompassed ancient archaeological sites and historic haciendas renovated for touristic consumption (Breglia 2009; Córdoba Azcárate, Garcia de Fuentes, and Córdoba Ordóñez 2014).

The promotion of archaeological sites through heritage tourism is a prominent strategy on the part of Mexican government agencies, namely the National Institute of Anthropology and History (INAH) and the Secretaria de Turismo de Mexico (National Secretary of Tourism, SECTUR) (Hutson, Can Herrera, and Chi 2014; Magnoni, Ardren, and Hutson 2007). The designation of several

DOI: 10.5876/9781607327721.c001

archaeological zones in the Maya World as World Heritage Sites through the United Nations Education, Science, and Culture Organization (UNESCO) has increased the scope of these promotions. UNESCO World Heritage Sites in the Maya World are, in order of inscription to the list, Tikal (1979), Copan (1980), Quirigua (1981), Palenque (1987), Chichén Itzá (1988), Joya de Cerén (1993), Uxmal (1996), and Calakmul (2002) (UNESCO 2017). Because nearly all of the forty-six sites on the Yucatán Peninsula, encompassing the Mexican states of Campeche, Yucatán, and Quintana Roo, are administered by INAH, the Mexican government is complicit in the policies made for the excavation and opening of sites to tourism. With the designation of sites on UNESCO's list, archaeological remains became more than patrimony of Mexico. They became the heritage of all the world's citizens.

Indigenous communities in Mexico and elsewhere are encouraged by state and federal governments to transform cultural and ecological resources into sites of tourist consumption (Ceballos-Lascurain 1987; Berger and Wood 2010; Van den Berghe 1995). In many ways, this is a form of tourism governance, though terms such as *tourism politics, policy, policy-making and planning,* and *destination management* are more commonly used in the literature (Bramwell and Lane 2011). Governance is more than just formal agencies of government involved in tasks. It includes non-state actors that are in the community, business, and voluntary sectors. Mexico's indigenous population—defined as native speakers of one of Mexico's sixty-five indigenous languages—constitutes 6.7 percent of the national population (INEGI 2009). The Mexican government identified indigenous tourism as an important vehicle for economic development in poor, marginalized communities that had the potential for developing their natural and cultural resources into tourist attractions (Villarreal 2014). This includes traditional cultural performances, diverse ecosystems, and archaeological zones.

Many factors have worked simultaneously since 2004 to make the village of Ek'Balam a destination. The agents engaged in the process include residents, funders, volunteers, missionaries, and tourists. These groups are traditionally divided into two categories in the literature on tourism: hosts and guests (Smith 1989). This model has been the foundation of most scholarly research on the tourism phenomenon, yet it constricts our ability to understand both sides of these tourism encounters. The host-guest dichotomy allows the guests a series of choices—such as what destination they visit, which type of tourism they engage in, and how much interaction they want to have with locals—while confining the host to a passive recipient of tourism and tourists. To gain a holistic understanding of this phenomenon, we must move beyond the "host-guest founding myth" (Aramberri 2001) to inform the much-needed creation of new theoretical paradigms for the study of tourism. We must base these paradigms on the assertion that the hosts are autonomous actors working within a politicized system rather than natives waiting to be duped (Stronza 2001).

Rather than hosts, I propose that residents of Ek'Balam are guides on this tour, as they have certainly been mine. Throughout the book, I present one family—the Ay Mena household—as a metaphor for understanding the countless ways residents pursue and experience tourism. We will first meet the Ay Mena family on a summer evening in 2004. In April of that year, residents opened the village's community-based tourism (CBT) project—known locally as "the Cabañas"—and welcomed their first guests. This was a long time in the making, and among the participating households there was a high level of excitement and enthusiasm as they received their first few guests. At the same time, the project drew on many of the community's resources. This fact was frustrating for the households not eligible to participate in the CBT project.

Throughout the book, we will visit the Ay Mena family seven times. Each visit provides a glimpse of a day in the life of this family at a specific point in time in relationship to the process of tourism development in the village. This is a fictive, composite family made up of the real actions and words of actual people in the community. It was difficult to determine how best to introduce these individuals to the reader. I decided that employing ethnographic allegory—or ethnographic realism as Oscar Lewis (1975) coined the phrase—would be the best way to both ensure their anonymity and provide a rich, thick description of the lived daily experiences residents have with tourists and tourism. This composite family of fictionalized individuals represents the real experiences of various residents.

Writing ethnography about a community of this size poses a variety of unique challenges. Because of the small population (approximately 350), the small number of households (approximately 75), and the even smaller number of large kin groups (7), simply assigning pseudonyms to members of a household would not adequately obscure their identities. Actual conversations and events that took place provided the basis for writing about the interactions within this composite family and among members of the family, other residents, and me. It is my hope that through the intimate portrait these vignettes provide, the reader will understand the nuanced ways residents engage with tourism, economic change, and the constant rotation of state and federal programs, missionaries, non-governmental organizations (NGOs), and tourists while still living their daily ives.

SUMMER 2004

Roosters do not wait until daybreak to crow and instead are clocks that mark the passing hours. The sound of barking dogs, startled from their sleep, and roosters crowing rings out throughout the night. Sunrise brings new sounds: men whistle to their dogs to head to the milpa, turkeys rustle and gobble as they leave their perches to begin the day, and radios announce the morning with intermittent static as women tune in the local station. On Saturday mornings the radios blare especially loudly, as people enjoy the four-hour Mayan-language program. As the fires are revived, the sounds of sleeping children join the cacophony. Smoke seeps out of kitchens and into the air, slowly at first, then more quickly as the cooking fires get going. Women heat water for Nescafe or Chocomilk, after which they will heat up some of last night's tortillas or, on some days, pull down the bag of assorted *pan dulce* (sweet bread).

On Tuesday and Saturday nights, a vendor from the bakery comes through Ek'Balam honking his horn and selling baked goods. A weekly purchase of *pan dulce* is stored out of reach of the animals in the hanging rack that, for a brief period of its existence, was the front guard of an oscillating fan. Everything has a use here, regardless of the manufacturer's suggestion. Fan guards double as hanging racks for storage out of the reach of small children and animals and as grills to place over the fire. Their shape conveniently mimics the size and shape of a *comal* (griddle), balanced on the three rocks of the fire for cooking tortillas. In the small one-room homes that are prone to mild flooding, nothing can be stored on the ground, and there must indeed be a place for everything. The thatch roof provides many opportunities for storage, aided by long iron hooks that hang at various lengths and hold burlap sacks, pots, buckets, and cardboard boxes.

On a lazy Saturday with the Ay Mena family in the summer of 2004, the whole house is in high spirits. I took the day off from my usual routine of walking around the village to talk to people and arrange interviews. Two months have passed, and we have all become accustomed to each other. Vanessa, the youngest child at six years old, asked me this morning if I could spend the day visiting with her instead of with other residents around town, so I happily complied and only left the house and yard a few times. The six children are animated and fooling around, playing between their two languages and only letting me in on the Maya when they are satisfied that I have searched my tiny vocabulary and cannot find the word. Doña Gomercinda and don Lucas keep up an occasional dialogue between themselves while still listening to everything we are saying. Residents use the prefixes "doña" and "don" to refer to all married women and men, respectively. These are honorific terms in reference to elderly people in some other parts of the country; however, they remain in common use in rural areas in Yucatán for married people of any age. Doña Gomercinda, my ever-present translator and source of all knowledge, interjects with explanations in Spanish when she sees that I cannot understand the rapid fire of Maya in short syllables and the raised voices reserved for antagonizing a sibling. Yucatec Maya is the residents' first language. When children go to school, they learn Spanish; however, Maya is still the predominant language for communication at home.

Eugenio, the eldest child at sixteen, is home from the neighboring city of Temozón for the weekend and is spending a rare evening in the house. He attends high school in Temozón and lives with his aunt, doña Florencia, only returning to the village on weekends. If he stays on this path, he will be the first young person from Ek'Balam to complete his education through high school. If a student wants to continue beyond the sixth grade, he or she must leave Ek'Balam for the neighboring towns of Santa Rita, Actuncóh, or Temozón. For study beyond the ninth grade, Temozón is the closest option. While these towns are not particularly far in terms of distance, the expense of clothes, transportation, and food away from home is prohibitive. Eugenio's continued education relies on his family's ability to make sacrifices to meet those expenses.

Dinner this evening consists of a family favorite, *ensalada* with salted pork. Temozón is locally famous for its smoked meats, sausages, and salted pork; and a trip through there is generally not complete without purchasing at least a half kilo of smoked, salted pork. Once home, the strips of smoked meat are diced and combined with cabbage, red onions, tomatoes, cilantro, and fresh lime juice to make a refreshing dinner on this hot summer night. Part of the children's animation is caused by Eugenio's presence and a great dinner, while the other part is excitement because the long school year is finally over. This means that slingshots, corn sack–shrouded forts, hopscotch, and a mountain of dirty clothes for doña Gomercinda to wash will fill the hot and sticky days.

Salvador, the second son, is twelve years old, excited to be heading into fifth grade in the fall. For him, the fact that school is out means more time to devote to his work at Hotel Eden, a hotel and restaurant in the village. Joan, the North American proprietor, keeps him and a handful of other young boys busy with gardening tasks and odd jobs. Hotel Eden opened in 2001 and received mixed responses from residents. While Joan is a controversial figure among some groups in the village, the Ay Mena family has a close relationship with her. Doña Goma works there as well, washing towels and linens three times a week. For his twelfth birthday last month, Salvador saved up his earnings and Joan matched what he had so he could buy a new bicycle. Salvador plans to go on to secondary and high school.

Rosa, the eldest daughter at thirteen, took the opposite route and left school after finishing sixth grade. She is content to have time to help her mother around the house, perfect her weaving techniques, and work from time to time in the kitchen of the community-based tourism development project. While Eugenio and Salvador are exceptions to the norm with regard to their pursuit of schooling, Rosa's decision to leave school after sixth grade is more typical of girls in the village.

The two younger boys, Federico and Ignacio (Nacho for short), are the family hams and keep everyone entertained, be it intentional or otherwise. They go everywhere together but are very different from one another. Each has attributes that are almost the opposite of the other. Federico is already suave at just eleven and an eager entertainer, while Nacho is practical, gruff, and a typical nine-year-old boy. When you see them walking together, arms thrown casually over each other's shoulder, they complement each other to such an extent that they sometimes seem like one boy.

The youngest is Vanessa, the smallest child with the biggest personality. I think often about how much I will enjoy seeing her as a young woman. At six years old, she is confident and often contrary, as she quite seriously tells you that it is cold if you comment on how hot the afternoon is. Unlike some other girls her age, Vanessa is bold when it comes to interacting with tourists. When she saw that I was making appointments with individuals to conduct interviews, she began insisting on appointments to play with me.

The kitchen house can hardly contain all of the family's energy, and the boys move in and out as they eat, joke, and then go into the main house to watch whatever is on the small black-and-white television. The smoke from the cooking fire drifts lazily out through the separated poles of the curved walls and up through the thatch roof and into the night air. The only constants during the meal are the patting sound of Rosa and doña Gomercinda making perfectly round tortillas. They sit at a small table next to the fire and turn out tortillas just as fast as the boys can eat them. Don Lucas sits at the larger table eating and conversing in his unique way of part Maya, part Spanish, all the while glancing at doña Gomercinda to fill in the spaces between words.

Don Lucas was born in the village of X'Kumil and moved to Ek'Balam with his family as a young man when the entire community relocated. His was one of the first families to make the move in 1969, and seven of his eight siblings still live in the village. He is a tall man, with a long, regal profile. His skin is very brown, and his thick black hair is just showing the first signs of gray near his temples. I spend much time observing don Lucas and find that he spends just as much time observing me. He notes every blister, bite, and scratch; and he fusses at doña Gomercinda when she does not notice or if she does not tell him when I am ill and not eating much. Don Lucas is an *ejidatario*—an individual with land rights in a given land grant community—and is one of the associates of the community-based tourism project. He enjoys most of the work he does for the project and trusts in the prospect of his participation being a good choice economically. The only part he does not enjoy is when guests arrive during his shift as night watchman.

Every twenty days, it is his turn to spend twenty-four hours at the Cabañas. He does some gardening and takes care of any pending tasks. He is also in charge of checking in any guests who arrive. Don Lucas, like the other twenty-three associates, does not speak English. His Spanish, as with twelve of the other associates, is broken at best. When guests do arrive, he has a difficult time communicating with them and attending to their needs. This interaction is uncomfortable and even embarrassing for him and translates as poor customer service from the guests' perspective. Still, he maintains that this project will improve and says he wants to keep participating so that once business does improve, his children will be able to work there. Like all the other families involved with the community-based tourism project, the Ay Mena household looks forward with great enthusiasm to the potential it holds. "They say it will be like a new Chichén Itzá, with gringos coming from all over the world to see the ruins," Lucas explains. This is a statement repeated regularly around the village. Everyone is waiting with bated breath for the onslaught of tourists, for better or worse.

Once everyone has finished their food, Eugenio leaves with his brothers not far behind. They will follow him on their bikes as far as he will permit, after which they will join the rest of the young boys playing soccer and riding their bikes around the plaza in the center of town. Doña Gomercinda, done making tortillas and satisfied that everyone has had enough to eat, joins us at the large green plastic table. She and Rosa are always the last to eat, though don Lucas lingers at the table or in the hammock until they finish. I sit with them on this night, enjoying the conversation we have settled into now that the younger children have left.

Doña Goma is entertaining us with a story about a family who came through that afternoon on the village tour. Joan started offering tours of the village to her guests last winter, and Goma's house is one of the main stops. According to her, this particular family has the biggest gringo baby she has ever seen. Residents use the slang term gringo (gringa in its feminine form) almost interchangeably with foreigner. In other parts of Mexico, this has a negative connotation, but in Ek'Balam they are simply classificatory terms. Goma often remarks on how big the children of gringo tourists are. The first question she asks in most encounters is how old the children are. Now that summer vacation is here, there are always children running in many directions. She often calls a local child over to compare the sizes of the two children. Her general conclusion as to why the gringos' children are so much larger is that the gringos are wealthy enough to take better care of their children. Her first reaction when a family comes on the tour is to touch the children and tell them to sit beside her if they seem uncertain. This is what she would do with any child, and it seems the logical response to making a timid child comfortable. She has learned, however, that often the parents seem uncomfortable with her doing this. They want to keep their children as far away as possible from the cooking fire, and they are not accustomed to strangers touching their children.

Doña Goma recognizes their discomfort and equates this with her feelings about photography. Tourists often take photos of children in the village, which was sometimes seen as evidence that they wanted to steal them. Many women deduced that they may give the photos to prospective adoptive parents. Joan has tried to quell some fears about photographs, but there is still a level of discomfort. For doña Goma, the fear is subsiding, in part because she has more interactions with tourists than do many other women in Ek'Balam. Between her work at Joan's and the village tour that stops at her house, she interacts with tourists on a regular basis. Some days she considers telling Joan that she can no longer host the tours. Often, she devotes hours to getting ready in case there will be a tour the next day. Guests in Hotel Eden's fourth year are still sporadic, so Joan can rarely give Goma much advance notice. This leaves her to fret about the ash and soot on the ceiling and the lack of adequate furniture to accommodate the gringos.

Once Goma has finished eating, she begins to put the food in small pails that hang from the thatch on long hooks, and she stacks the dishes on the table to wash in the morning. Always the last to bathe, she pours hot water into a bucket and disappears into the bathhouse. All of the children and don Lucas have taken their baths and left a pile of dirty clothes in the bathhouse. She calls out to no one in particular: "Very nice. Now I'll spend all day tomorrow washing clothes and there will be nothing to eat." This elicits a response from Vanessa and Nacho, who have returned from playing and are settling in their hammocks. Nacho grumbles that he will kill a dove with his slingshot and cook it himself. Vanessa, overtired from the day, begins to cry, says she will be hungry tomorrow, and calls for her mother to come to bed.

Everyone sleeps in the one-room thatch house next to the kitchen. Hung from the beams are four brightly colored hammocks. Goma and Vanessa sleep in one, Lucas and Federico in another, and Nacho, Rosa, and Salvador in a third. The fourth hammock is mine, and as much as I argue that I would be happy to sleep in the kitchen, everyone insists that there is plenty of room. Finally, doña Goma finishes her bath and comes into the house. Lucas closes up the kitchen and turns off the lights, then shuts the back door of the house but does not tie the rope to secure it. Federico has returned, but Salvador is still out riding his new bike. Eugenio is out with friends and will probably not be back for some time. When Lucas is satisfied that everything is in its place, he turns off the light and settles in to watch television with the rest of us. The television rests on a shelf near the ceiling where everyone can see it, and we all drift off to sleep watching the dramatic, opulent, black-and-white lives of characters in the current soap opera.

APPROACH

This book is an ethnographic case study of one village's experience with community-based tourism (CBT) development. My goal in writing this book is to contribute to our understanding of how a group of people negotiates and maneuvers through a web of social programs, tourists, volunteers, and external expectations to live their daily lives. In this milieu, potential for development is everywhere. Against the backdrop of the constant rotation of state and federal programs implemented to aid Mexico's poor, indigenous, rural citizens—its *campesinos*—tourism arrives as the new "Proyecto (Project)." A resident once asked me, "What is your project?" I explained that I was conducting research and did not have a specific project. He replied, "Well, everybody has a project. You should just pick one."

The focus of this research is the CBT project U Najil Ek'Balam. While many other projects of various scopes and intentions came and went during the course of my fieldwork, the CBT project was the constant. Discussions about the variety of other "projects" with residents and agency staff informed this research; however, I present these data only insofar as they relate specifically to the CBT project. This longitudinal study provides a view of one community's engagement with tourism, development, and change over an eight-year period. In the process of conducting this fieldwork, I began to see patterns in the design and implementation of the various development projects, which included school improvement, adobe stoves, cultural revitalization, payments for forest conservation, and many more. The residents participating were eligible to do so because of the groups or categories they occupy. Some projects target women, while farmers have access to others. There are projects implemented with cultural preservation as their main objective and others whose goal is to modernize some aspect of daily life. Many of these projects require individuals to be indigenous, technologically perceptive, or adamant conservationists, for example. One of the problematic issues with these requirements is that the project design rarely accounts for the fact that residents of Ek'Balam, like people everywhere, do not fall within any one category.

Scholars in Yucatán and Mesoamerica more broadly long ago rejected the concept of the folk-urban continuum for its oversimplification of what we know to be cultural realities and its insistence on the ethnographic present. This refers to the tendency in early anthropological writings to present a culture as something separate from its historical context and current processes of change. The question that remains is whether we can successfully move beyond ideas such as the folk-urban continuum if we continue to replace it with an array of tourism continuums. We define destinations as un-toured or tourist-ed or as having nascent tourism development versus being "overrun." We categorize their location on or off the beaten path. Instead, I argue that we need to position these "little communities" as part of a larger social, political, and economic system and approach tourism in a similar way to how we understand any other aspect of life in rural Yucatán. To provide a holistic view of this community, I focus on the economics of agrarian reform and local household production, the community's social structure, and the politics of indigeneity and authenticity in the context of tourism development.

While the presence of millions of tourists in the Maya World certainly complicates the debate over what exactly we mean by "Maya," it has been going on since long before Cancún transformed from a sand spit in the Caribbean to the well-known destination it is today. The interest in and importance of heritage in the context of a tourism-driven economy does necessitate the identification of heirs and thus the use of identity politics to determine the modern-day heirs of Maya culture (Castañeda 2004; Gabbert 2004). The scholarship on identity in the Maya World can be roughly divided into two groups: constructivists and essentialists (Medina 2003). Essentialists argue for cultural continuity between ancient and modern expressions of Maya-ness. For them, a Maya person living today is a clear descendant of a resident of one of the hundreds of ancient Maya cities throughout the region.

Another version of this debate is presented by Edward F. Fischer (2001), who separates essentialism from anti-essentialism. He defines essentialism as "analysis that is simplistic or universal in its assumptions" (Fischer 2001, 9). He goes on to discuss the Redfieldian propensity for the use of trait lists, which essentializes individuals and groups by reducing the diversity of lived experience to mere categories. In contrast, Fischer (2001, 10) sums up the anti-essentialist approach with his assertion that "what we know about the Maya, or any other group, is ultimately distilled from what we know about particular individuals, a knowledge that is at best incomplete." The constructivist and anti-essentialist arguments surrounding Maya identity are broadly a critique of the notion that the modern and ancient Maya shared cultural traits. Peter Hervik (1999) refers to this notion as the reification of daily life through ethnographic work in Yucatán.

To move past a discussion of Maya as an essential identity, Ronald Loewe (2010, 61) suggests that the political syncretism of *mestizaje* become the foundation for analysis to understand "how ethnic groups relate to one another structurally as well as symbolically." Similarly, other scholars (Mallon 1995; Reyes-Foster 2012) discuss the way a nationalist ideology is developed both from the top down (i.e., concepts of how to deal with indigenous populations) and from within these populations (i.e., what it means for a resident of a rural village to be a proper citizen). Finally, Fernando Armstrong-Fumero (2012) concludes that people in this part of Mexico used identity politics in similar ways in the twentieth-century agrarian struggles and the twenty-first-century challenges of neo-liberalization and multiculturalism by determining which of their multiple identities—peasant, Maya, indigenous—would be the most powerful in any given context. My approach to these questions in the context of essentialism, constructivism, and the state management of ethnic groups is to rely on rich, thick description and ethnographic detail of daily life in one community to understand how members of the community define themselves.

This research did not produce a picture postcard of a day in the life; rather, I focused on the active processes in which residents choose to participate. Instead of selecting the way the arrival of tourism affects residents as the object of study, I present a story about this arrival onto the already lush landscape of everyday life. With this arrival comes a shift in the perception and execution of numerous aspects of everyday life. Suddenly, heritage is all around. Homes have become cultural markers, and the forest is an attraction. The ubiquitous nature of heritage has created in Ek'Balam a drive to provide the authentic: to create and maintain an ecosystem of authenticity.

AN ECOSYSTEM OF AUTHENTICITY

Anthropologists have employed the concept of an ecosystem in their work in varying ways. Early uses from around the 1960s are attributed to both a rejection of the earlier environmental determinism and the use of biological concepts to take some of the burden off the concept of culture (Morán 1990). The resurgence of interest in ecosystems as a framework for anthropological inquiry views them as complex adaptive systems (Abel and Stepp 2003). The systems approach enables us to consider both internal and external influences, including development agencies and regional economic forces, such as tourism. This holistic approach to understanding this particular environment and the people who inhabit it is integral to understanding how local resources are managed in indigenous villages throughout Yucatán (Anderson 2005; Faust, Anderson, and Frazier 2004).

While generally used in reference to an ecological system, the concept lends itself to the metaphorical way I use the concept of an "ecosystem of authenticity" throughout this book. An early definition of ecosystem is one in which there is an ongoing exchange "not only between the organisms, but also between the organic and the inorganic" (Tansley 1935, 299). Thick forests, barren fields, conservation initiatives, tourism development strategies, and archaeological remains all define the ecosystem in which residents of Ek'Balam reside. It is home to people who are in constant negotiation with the idea of authenticity and who have an array of notions about how to generate and maintain it. As we will see through their stories, providing an authentic Maya village is dependent on multiple factors: houses should look a certain way, individuals should dress a certain way, men should farm their land and actively conserve the parts they are not farming, women should grind corn on a *metate* and weave hammocks. The list of correct behavior is long, and the task of following these prescriptions for authenticity is a conscious, active choice made by residents every day.

A variety of people from all over the world visit Ek'Balam. Some are on a brief getaway from their all-inclusive resort vacation on the coast, while others are eco-tourists planning to enjoy two weeks of quiet in the village. Still others come as part of a number of volunteer opportunities or with their church group. What they have in common is that they are not tourists, regardless of how it may appear. In fact, they are working hard to inform themselves about their destinations and the people and experiences they will encounter there. In the case of volunteer tourists and missionaries, they are paying for their stay with both currency and labor. They are willing to pay more and forego many luxuries in their quest for authenticity of experience. What is the benchmark of this authenticity? No tourists allowed. Dean MacCannell (1976, 9) also recognized this sentiment and wrote that "it is intellectually chic nowadays to deride tourists." An apt illustration of this sentiment is expressed in his citation of Claude Lévi-Strauss's statement that "travel and travelers are two things I loathe—and yet here I am, all set to tell the story of my expeditions" (quoted in MacCannell 1976, 9). The discourse surrounding tourist perceptions of other tourists always contains something about "the beaten path," which is avoided by all. The following excerpt from an interview with a husband and wife staying in Ek'Balam illustrates this desire for an experience the typical visitor perceives as different or more authentic:

D: Another thing that was really great was to bring [our son] to a place like this that was really untouched and not spoiled by commercialism, and surrounded by a village of native people so that he could get a real sense of what the natural beauty of the place was like and what the real sense of it is without the gift stores, the tour busses, without all of that and without it being touched. To get a feel of what the area is like.

J: Yeah, we're not real tourist folks. We prefer to be in a village or to be with a family, or to be in a place like this here where we're still part of it. If you're going to go to the jungle, there is no sense in staying in a resort where they close the gates and say, "don't go outside because the people are bad" and you have to stay there and spend your money there. Instead of a pool, I would rather swim in a *cenote*, you know?

[Transcriptions: 2007-0627 (22:07)]

For some, tourism provides a respite from their inauthentic everyday lives (Brown 2013); however, the main component of this authentic experience is, in fact, the everyday lives of inhabitants of the destination (Rickly-Boyd 2013). Residents of Ek'Balam are familiar with the sentiments expressed here. Repeated tourist encounters, discussions with visiting staff members from the agency funding the CBT project, and the media, with which residents are highly engaged, regularly reinforce the desires these and most other visitors bring with them. Strong images and associations are contained and transmitted in narratives such as this. Residents are acutely aware of the contexts tourists ask to photograph—a girl in traditional dress, a woman weaving, or a thatch-roof house—and actively engage in the reproduction of these images (Cant 2015). The idea that Ek'Balam is "untouched and not spoiled by commercialism" and the association of "native people" with "natural beauty" are just a few of the ideals and expectations residents mold themselves to fit as part of touristic performance.

While this mandate of government-sponsored Maya-ness is communicated to purveyors of tourism destinations and commodities, it is met in contrasting ways within the development of mass tourism in urban settings and the development of adventure or eco-tourism in rural areas. The common theme is authenticity. In creating and maintaining a typical Maya village, residents are increasingly preoccupied with defining exactly what is authentic. All of this brings us to the ever-elusive question of authenticity. Is there a difference between traditions that are maintained in relative isolation from tourists and those that are performed specifically for tourists? Does the authenticity of one render the other inauthentic? Conflicting views on these questions are found in the literature on tourism (Medina 2003). According to MacCannell (1976), staged authenticity ceases to fall into the category of an authentic cultural expression. Erik Cohen (1988) disagrees and discusses a new category for such performances: "emergent authenticity."

In many ways, the authenticity debate from tourism studies overlaps with the identity debate found in Maya ethnology (Medina 2003). Identity is often at the foundation of tourism studies in Mesoamerican communities, such as Walter E. Little's (2004b) concept of performing tourism and, in turn, Maya identity. Ronda I. Brulotte's (2012) use of MacCannell's reconstructed ethnicity in examining the nationalist paradigm that equates rural craft production with indigeneity among Oaxacan artisans is another example of this. This "reconstructed ethnicity" is a response to the pressures of cultural performance, as mandated by the tourism encounter (Brulotte 2009).

While the notion of an ecosystem is of something inclusive, it can be broken down into two parts: the physical surroundings and the people who inhabit them. As such, my research took a two-pronged approach. I first set out to understand how households in the community balance economic strategies that prioritize tourism—such as handicraft production, biodiversity conservation, and the provision of accommodations—with traditional economic strategies for land use, which is mainly production of maize for subsistence. The second task was to understand the relationship between economic and ecological decision-making processes and the local social structure of kinship, specifically with regard to its correlation with a household's ability to benefit from local tourism development.

It is at this interface that transnational ideologies of ecological conservation and sustainable economic development complicate the local-level tension between tourism and tradition. Given these conflicts, can community-based tourism be a viable avenue to sustainable development? This book presents a discussion of the strategies employed by residents to negotiate the design and management of a CBT project in the midst of everyday life. Residents turn to markers of indigeneity in response to external demands, including maintenance of an image of rurality, increased valuation of traditional ecological knowledge (TEK), and staged ritual performance. Because the degree to which an individual engages these strategies is dependent on the person's social position within the community, the choice to incorporate them into everyday life is a political one. The recognition of the political, intentional nature of these strategies is what makes the conceptual framework of the ecosystem of authenticity a viable replacement for the continuums previously mentioned.

ORGANIZATION OF THE BOOK

This first chapter of the book brings the reader to the two Ek'Balams: the archaeological zone and the adjacent village. Chapter 2 introduces the various forces at work locally and at the regional level that are influencing the social, political, and economic life of this small town. After meeting the Ay Mena family again on a summer afternoon in 2006, the reader learns about the history of both the village and the project. This chapter also discusses the methods used in the research and positions me, the researcher, as a participant in the daily life of the village.

Chapter 3 contextualizes Ek'Balam's CBT project in the existing literature about tourism, development, and indigeneity and provides a theoretical framework for the research. During the summer 2007 visit with the Ay Mena family, we learn about some of the ongoing projects in the community and the ever-increasing presence of young volunteers in the village. With the realization that there are major structural issues underlying the development of tourism in Ek'Balam, chapter 4 walks the reader through the pertinent history of agrarian reform in the region and the neo-liberal policy shifts that have changed so many things at the local and national levels. There have been some major changes in the country's land tenure system, and the visit with the Ay Mena family in December 2008 presents opinions about what people should and should not do with their land.

Chapter 5 addresses the community development aspect of the research. With the realization that this seemingly homogeneous peasant/rural/indigenous community is actually a stratified social structure rife with elite domination and other initially invisible characteristics of relative poverty, the reader is ready to learn more about how this project is playing out within the ejidal system. When we see the Ay Mena family in July 2009, we find them in the midst of crisis and learn that this crisis is felt throughout the community. The primary goals of the CBT project and the rest of the various development initiatives in the community are an improved standard of living and a socially and economically sustainable plan for the future. What we find in 2009 is anything but sustainable.

The sixth chapter brings together what readers already know about the community and challenges them to reconcile that knowledge with what they think they know. This chapter employs examples of various performances to help us reframe concepts such as Maya-ness, indigeneity, and traditional culture. The aim of this chapter is to gain an understanding of the articulation of the tactics locals use and the strategies state actors use in the process of building and managing a tourism project. The state employs strategies that reinforce the importance of performance for tourists, while locals resort to tactics that conceal cosmopolitanism but allow them to remain competent in the eyes of funders. These development endeavors problematize concepts such as verticality, encompassment, and governmentality. The desire of state agents to designate and market "local" leads to situations in which the individuals defined as such are expected to exist in concurrent states of authenticity and modernity, as traditional and cosmopolitan.

Chapter 7 is a discussion of the overall success of tourism development in the community. Development projects are evaluated using a variety of means; however, in the case of Ek'Balam, some of these evaluations are more efficient than others. This is particularly important in this case because of the varying perspectives of different kin groups and households in the community. The book concludes by asking readers to reflect on the frequent use of continuums in anthropological writing and to ask themselves how exactly it is that we account for so much variety in individual choices having to do with how exactly one should inhabit his or her assigned space on the continuum. Other scholars have talked about tourism border zones as empty meeting grounds; however, this ethnographic case study challenges this by introducing readers to a community of people who are, by any definition, living life at many points on the continuum.

The chapters culminate in a map of the ecosystem of authenticity as imagined by residents of Ek'Balam. Starting with a micro-level focus and then zooming out to the macro-level affords readers an understanding of one of the main tenets of the book: this community is neither isolated nor overrun, neither traditional nor modern. Instead, this community consists of a wide array of perspectives and people actively involved in daily negotiations with tourists, volunteers, state and federal funders, and each other. It is through these negotiations and their perceptive, intentional maneuvering that residents are able to be Maya and get by.

Maps, Guides, and the Beaten Path

RAFAEL: "What book is that, the one you are reading?"
SARAH: "This? It's a dictionary, a Maya-English dictionary."
RAFAEL: "Ahh, I thought it was a book like the ones the *gringos* always look at."
SARAH: "What book is it that they always look at?"
RAFAEL: "*Quien sabe*? [Who knows] But they're big and always have lots of maps. Maybe if we had some maps more *gringos* would come here."

[TRANSCRIPTIONS 2004-0812 (2:01)]

According to most residents of Ek'Balam, gringos love maps. They spend much of their time reading from large books and looking at maps. Locals use maps in the specific context of land dealings, but apart from this, most residents do not use maps at all. Many have never seen a two-dimensional, bird's-eye view of the spaces they inhabit.

Maps occupy a very special place in the anthropological process. In early ethnographies from around the world, the map of the village or region was one of the first pieces of information given to readers. Maps remain an important

DOI: 10.5876/9781607327721.c002

component of many more recent monographs on Mesoamerica as well. Tourists have a different relationship with maps. One of the most important qualities that attract visitors to Ek'Balam is its location off the beaten path. Interestingly, these very books provide a map to aid the traveler in leaving the so-called beaten path without getting lost.

The maps of Ek'Balam that do exist are visual representations of the archaeological zone's monumental center. There are no maps of the town or of the town's relationship to the archaeological zone. The content of the archaeological site map is logical, as a map that delineates the roads and major points of interest in the modern settlement of Ek'Balam would be. When I set out to meet Rafael's request for a map, we sketched the roads first. Things became complicated when we started adding features and gaining volunteers with varied opinions on what a good map of the village should convey. The list of important attributes grew and changed depending on whom we encountered. Ultimately, it became clear that this map was as much a visual representation of residents' ideologies as a delineation of the physical features of the village. The same list of correct behavior that dictates how individuals and households must present themselves to tourists slowly manifested in the various iterations of the map. What we had at the end was not a map of the village of Ek'Balam but instead a map of residents' visions of all the features that are part of Ek'Balam and its ecosystem of authenticity.

For some travelers, a destination with no map is a touristic dream come true. Upon arrival in Ek'Balam, though, even the most seasoned travelers may feel lost. If they are guests at the CBT project, they are removed from the town. Guests at any of the hotels are unsure about walking around the village in the evening because they do not know what is out there. They saw the main road into town, made a quick right turn followed by a left and another right, and arrived at their destination. If, as in the case of Antigua, Guatemala, "the preponderance of maps undermines the tourist experience," what does a dearth of maps mean for tourists in Ek'Balam (Little 2004b, 67)? Various maps provide views of Ek'Balam throughout the chapters of this book. All of these maps are the product of a mapping project conducted by community members and myself between 2010 and 2012 in response to Rafael's statement that perhaps a map was what had been missing. This chapter is a map of three aspects of this research: the local social structure as organized around kinship, the methodological approach I took, and the historical context of Ek'Balam that led to the current nature of everyday life in the village.

SUMMER 2006

The past winter holiday season should have been a prosperous time for residents of Ek'Balam engaged in tourism. The Cabañas (the local, federally funded community-based tourism [CBT] project) had been open for more than a year and was starting to attract visitors, and Hotel Eden was looking forward to its busiest season yet. An Italian couple was constructing a large hotel in the middle of town and providing some work for locals in the process. Unfortunately, two huge hurricanes came through in September 2005 and nearly destroyed those businesses. The CBT project had to replace six of the nine thatch roofs and the storm demolished Hotel Eden's towering *palapa* roof, forcing it to close for more than six months. Hotel Eden's closure left doña Goma without the additional income of the village tour and her work doing laundry at the hotel. Other commodities were in short supply as well. The construction of the CBT project required a large commitment of time and materials from all twenty-six associates. They all brought palms from their parcels for the thatch roofs, which left very little for their own roofs that also needed repair after the hurricane.

By the summer, cleanup looks to be under way, and things are returning to normal. The lasting reminders of the storms are the many identical new houses scattered around the village. The new blockhouses came as part of a government program. Almost every household received materials for a house, and most were constructed alongside the existing pole-and-thatch structures. Before the storms, there were very few houses constructed of block in the village. Many of the households that elected to have a blockhouse are not actually occupying them. Instead, they accepted the materials and built the houses as a plan for their futures. The Ay Mena family constructed the blockhouse for one of the sons to bring his wife to live in when the time comes.

The construction of the new blockhouse changed the look of the Ay Menas' yard, but it also created a lovely place under their large Almendra tree to sit and enjoy the shade. Lucas and Goma are enjoying a moment of rest and a cold Coca Cola and recounting the destruction the hurricanes wrought and the many changes that have come in their wake. Lucas is still participating in the CBT project, but he worries about its long-term success because in the past six months the number of associates has dwindled from twenty-six to eighteen. He says that many of them became frustrated at having to invest so many resources without any return. What began in 2001 as a project set to benefit the community as a whole was beginning to encounter difficulty in the relationship between the associates and the community. Particularly in the wake of the brutal storms, many feel the project is failing to benefit the community and is only ever going to be something for local elites.

The Cabañas consist of nine *palapas*—thatch-roof, one-room structures— built in the style of the thatch houses in the village but reinforced with plaster and paint on the inside walls. Each of the three large *palapas* has two rooms with bathrooms inside; the remaining six are each one large room with a bathroom in a separate structure just a few steps from the back door. Each room boasts multiple beds in king and twin sizes, ample mosquito netting, screened windows, flush toilets, and ceiling fans—amenities not found in any houses in the village. The process of appointing the rooms was challenging for the residents participating in the tourism project and, according to some of the leaders, they were grateful for the advice of their sponsors because of their lack of experience with tourists and in general with anything to do with a hotel. The average age of the men working on this project is forty-five, and of the eighteen participants, only three had ever stayed in a hotel.

On the east side of the Cabañas compound is the kitchen and dining area, under a grand thatch roof. The kitchen is built from stone and has all the amenities found in a commercial kitchen, including a large gas range the cooks especially enjoy working with. The dining area can hold nearly seventy-five people and overlooks a *chaltun*, or low area full of rocks, tall trees, and iguanas lazing away the day. The many trees in the *chaltun* and interspersed throughout the structures have painted white trunks, and a stroll through the cement walking paths connecting the various *palapas* reveals signs hung on the trees with their scientific, Spanish, and Maya names. On the other side of the road are the reception structure, a large open-air theater and stage, and a ceremonial steam bath, or *temezcal*. The men who participate in the project still take twenty-four-hour turns as guards to perform repairs; tend the gardens, lawn, and pool; and check guests in and out of the hotel. Now that there are fewer associates, Lucas explains that he has to spend nearly twice as many nights there. Every afternoon when the shift changes, a group of men sit on rocks outside the reception structure, talking about what needs to be done at the hotel and catching the last guard up on the events of the day in the village.

Commentary from the older boys, who think Lucas should drop out of the project, punctuates our conversation about the trials and triumphs of the CBT project. Among the households that have resigned from the project are two of Lucas's brothers. I ask if this means that he, too, will leave the project, but he explains that while they are members of the same family, each household generally makes its own decisions when it comes to things like this. Lucas and his family are not the only residents experiencing tension. Goma is also dealing with jealousy from other women in the community. When Joan was finally able to reopen Hotel Eden, she came to ask Goma to work right away. She knew there would be no training needed, and she also knew that Goma's outgoing personality would mean guests would have a good time and spread the word. Hotel Eden was in desperate need of an increase in business to recover financially from the storms and maintain the hotel and grounds.

The job prospects in and around Ek'Balam are slim, even with the recent development of a local tourism sector. Eugenio is discussing his concern that once he finishes high school in Temozón in two years, he will have to leave the village to find work. One of the primary objectives of the CBT project in the village is to keep young men from needing to migrate for work. According to Eugenio, the fact that he will have to leave town to find work instead of being able to work at the Cabañas is a prime example of why the project is a failure.

Maria del Rosario is quietly listening to our conversation while weaving alongside Goma. Her hammocks are better and better each time I see them, and she has been able to augment the household income with their sales. Rosa turned fifteen in June and the family threw a large—and very expensive—*quinceñera* (fifteenth birthday celebration) for her. Her brothers are beginning to tease her about finding a boyfriend, but she is not interested.

Salvador is disappointed that he cannot work at Joan's this summer but is still determined to continue school. He will graduate from the sixth grade next month and go on to junior high in Temozón in the new school year. Salvador is as soft-spoken and diplomatic as ever—the family peacekeeper. He interrupts Eugenio and tells him it is everyone's own choice to participate in the CBT project, migrate to the coast, and continue their studies. "Each head is a world," he reminds his older brother. This is a common saying, though it is more often heard from people much older than Salvador. The idea that each person makes up his or her own mind and that it is not possible for someone else to understand exactly how or why the individual does so is reflected in many interactions between family members and residents more broadly. Eugenio cannot say much to counter his little brother's observation.

Federico and Ignacio return from the backyard where they had been mending the chicken coop. Both are excited to see that their cousin Baltazar is there for a visit but are disappointed to find that there is no more Coca Cola. Baltazar is Lucas's sister's son and a regular presence at his aunt and uncle's house. He has been working in Cancún for about six months, ever since his father dropped out of the CBT project. The boys convince their little sister Vanessa to run down the street and get another cold two-liter bottle for them to enjoy. She protests, but Eugenio convinces her with two extra pesos so she can buy a piece of candy. Federico is thirteen and listens intently to his older cousin's stories about Cancún. He wants to finish school as quickly as possible and go have adventures on the coast. Baltazar encourages him to stay in school so he can get a better job. He says that if he is educated and can speak English, an entirely different sector of jobs could be open to him, and he would not be confined to just construction, plumbing, or other manual labor. Ignacio (Nacho for short) has no time for his cousin's counsel. For him, learning English so he can work on the coast is futile, since he wants to end up working here in the village like his father. At age eleven, he is certain that a life of farming is about the best thing he can imagine.

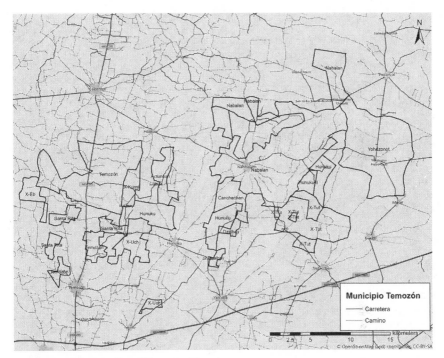

FIGURE 2.1. *Municipality of Temozón, Yucatán*

MAPPING EK'BALAM

The village of Ek'Balam is located in the municipality of Temozón (figure 2.1), inside the *ejido* of X'Kumil—one of thirteen in the municipality.

The political leaders in Ek'Balam and Temozón have varying levels of involvement with each other, depending mainly on the relationship between the president of the municipality and the village's municipal commissioner at a given time. These elected political offices change at the same time every three years. The social connections with the town of Temozón are much stronger than the political or economic ties. Many individuals in the village have family in Temozón, and young men from Ek'Balam often marry women from this neighboring community, creating multiple social links to families in Temozón.

The road into Ek'Balam is only wide enough for one car in most spots and is lined on either side by milpas, or cornfields. In the distance you can see *monte alto* (high forest), but close to the road it is obvious that the land has not been fallow for more than a few years at a time. The road ends at the village's central plaza (figure 2.2). The first house you see upon entering is that of doña Ima and her family. Next to the road, they have a small open structure with a thatch roof, under which hang hammocks woven in a riot of colors. Upon entering the

FIGURE 2.2. *Village of Ek'Balam, 2012*

village, the remnants of the abandoned hacienda around which Ek'Balam was founded can still be seen woven through the plaza in the center of the village. The concrete Catholic Church is built on a raised foundation where the grand house of the hacienda once stood. The well remains visible next to a water tank, to the west of the brightly painted town hall, or commissary building. An old stone wall of the hacienda separates the playground area from the church and empty space, and beneath the many Flamboyan trees (*Delonix regia*) you can still see the rock walls that cordoned off the garden of the hacienda grounds. Rather than a traditional central plaza, Ek'Balam has a square of land in the center of town with four sections: the church, the kiosk and playground, the commissary building, and an empty area crisscrossed with walking paths. Behind the town hall, or commissary, is the heart of the village. Children use this concrete slab— *la cancha*—for pickup soccer games that start as soon as school is out and last well into the night. Next to *la cancha* is a concrete gazebo surrounded by four benches. In the afternoon this is a place where little girls play hopscotch, and in the evening men slowly move over to the benches to visit with each other and catch up on the news of the day. Huge Ceiba (*Ceiba pentandra*) and Flamboyan trees surround the town center.

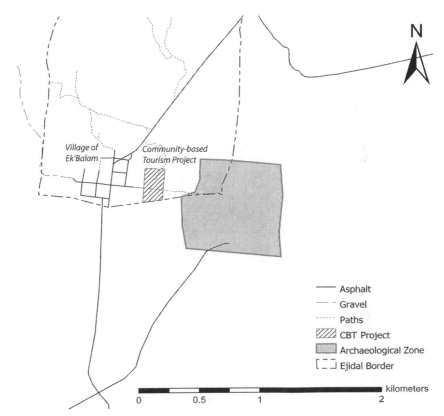

FIGURE 2.3. *Map of CBT project in relation to village*

The road continues around the main square of the plaza, past houses of pole and thatch and others of cement block. One block into the village, the road crosses another. A turn to the right (north) leads to the original entrance to the archaeological zone and is one of the five ancient roads of the old city. Just off this road is Hotel Eden, a foreign-owned hotel that opened in 2001. Joan, the proprietor, has created an impressive oasis of tropical plants, thatch-roof Cabañas, an inviting pool, and a menu of vegetarian Maya-inspired cuisine on her acre of land in Ek'Balam. The road continues west through the village toward the original entrance to the archaeological zone. The pavement ends and the road becomes a dirt road for a stretch before turning into a thin cattle trail that disappears into the forest, just past the town's community-based tourism project (figure 2.3): a hotel called U Najil Ek'Balam (House of the Black Jaguar).

The ethnographic fieldwork for this book took place between 2004 and 2012. During these eight years, I spent time in the village of Ek'Balam, at the archaeological zone, and in the neighboring town of Temozón. Ethnography provides an opportunity to collect data on the history, daily life, and lived experiences of this community too nuanced to document through surveys and census collection. These fine-grained data gave me the ability to present a micro-level analysis of the tourism development process. I also used statistical and census data from the Instituto Nacional de Estadistica y Geografia (National Institute of Statistics and Geography, INEGI).

My engagement with residents of Ek'Balam is characterized by a series of negotiations in various social fields. This is true for most ethnographers, but the reason I include an explicit discussion of these negotiations is that the definition of these social fields and the way people negotiate with each other in and between them is at the foundation of my research. Because this research is in the context of nascent tourism development and I myself look like a tourist to both locals and visitors, it is important for me to highlight from this early point the multiple roles I occupy in Ek'Balam: tourist, volunteer, anthropologist, student, teacher, gringa, and friend.

In May 2004 I was an undergraduate at California State University, Chico, when I had the opportunity to head south to Yucatán for the summer to conduct independent research on tourism and cultural change. I expected that I would find a village, and I would be respectful in my manner and diligent in my field notes and ask people what they thought of tourists and how their lives had been impacted by this phenomenon. At the end of the summer, I would have conducted twenty interviews and all of the answers to my questions would have been recorded on my trusty Dictaphone. This image, of course, bore little resemblance to the way the summer actually unfolded.

That first summer I thought the Flamboyan trees were some of the most beautiful things I had ever seen. Their brilliant orange flowers bunched at the end of every branch, and their delicate leaves danced in the afternoon breeze. Sitting in a cherished patch of shade in the afternoon, watching the flowers float to the ground and noticing the contrast between the nearly fluorescent orange and the clear blue sky that refused to rain, quickly became my favorite pastime. There I would sit, under the Flamboyanes in the center of town—hyper aware of every pore as a sheen of sweat developed on my back, arms, and face—and write up my notes each day. At first I sat alone and watched men returning from their milpas on bicycles, their dogs close behind. I watched children running back to their houses after the school bell rang and women returning from the maize grinder on paths across the grassy field. Shortly, I gained children who would come and watch me watch the village. They began to talk to me, and by the second week a whole bevy of children tailed my every move—just in time for me to find out that some of the women thought that I, a childless woman from the United States, was there to steal a child.

On the day I first arrived in Ek'Balam, I had the great good fortune to meet Gomercinda Ay Mena, who became my caretaker, cultural liaison, translator, and advocate. Her voice stood out among those of women who were uncertain of my intentions. In their eyes she spoke from a place of authority; she actually had the gringa living in her house. I stayed with the Ay Mena family that summer and every time I have been there since. Though I did not realize it at the time, I could not have chosen a better family to stay with, thereby aligning myself with them. They hold a neutral position in local politics, and while they are participating in the CBT project, don Lucas, Gomercinda's husband, is never in a leadership position. Doña Goma is rarely the subject of gossip around the village. No one in the family is known for drinking to excess, and most residents regard don Lucas as a hardworking man from one of the founding village families. The roles members of the Ay Mena family play in village life directly affected my ability to understand the nuanced social fabric of this small town.

Three years passed before doña Goma told me her version of my arrival story. Having a gringa living in your house was not easy in Ek'Balam, particularly during my first summer there in 2004 when tourists were still a spectacle. She always told me that if other women started asking about the particulars of my arrangement with her, I should just let them wonder or act as though I did not understand them. As time went on, I became friends with many families who regularly invited me in to visit during my daily walks around the village. By the summer of 2007, I found myself realizing that when women saw that I had learned how to make tortillas, they inevitably asked if I would ever come back. Many were doubtful when I explained that I would. The connection between my hard-won tortilla-making skills and my return was not apparent to me at first.

Finally, I asked Goma about this, and she laughed and laughed. She explained that during that first summer, she told them that I just pulled up in a taxi in front of her house and asked if she would teach me how to make tortillas in exchange for an occasional purchase of beans or produce. When she agreed, I unloaded my things and never left. While the influx of even small purchases into the household economy is welcome and helpful, the fact that I was not giving her money directly squelched some of the jealousy. Her story further positioned me in the innocuous role of a student, as someone who only came to learn this one skill. This undoubtedly affected to some degree the way other residents perceived me and interacted with me in the beginning.

ARRIVING IN EK'BALAM

As we will see throughout this study, things are not always as they seem. This Maya community is not a discrete unit but is instead a group of households with disparate views on many things, not the least of which is what is authentic. For many, authenticity includes structures, attire, and foodways. For others, authenticity is primarily a way of interacting with the natural environment. This group sees agriculture as the seminal marker of being an authentic *campesino*, or peasant farmer, and feels that other things are less foundational. Still others imagine authenticity as represented through the built environment and want to transform Ek'Balam into an ideological extension of the monumental center of the archaeological zone. The construction and maintenance of this ecosystem of authenticity is a contentious process that necessitates an examination of the groups involved.

The variation in the prescription for being Maya and the construction of authenticity presented a methodological conundrum. A short time after my arrival in Ek'Balam, it became clear to me that the primary organizational structure in the community was kinship. I learned quickly that every resident was a member of one of seven kin groups and that each of these groups had been in existence in the community since 1939, when they began the petition for their *ejidal* land grant. I found myself exploring a web of social and familial relationships, economic strategies, and varied resource management connected by a place. Given the active compliance with and resistance to this on the part of residents, interpretation is the most effective way to hear the many voices that make up this ecosystem.

Because of the longitudinal nature of this study, it was important to collect quantitative data to complement the qualitative data collected through participant observation and interviews. This created benchmarks by which I could measure change between 2004 and 2012. My initial attempts to collect these data consisted of casual conversations and a sort of snowball sampling (Bernard 2011), in which individuals I already knew introduced me to others whom I could ask the same questions. My interactions with residents were initially limited to members of the Ay Mena household, with whom I was staying; the municipal commissioner, or mayor; and the *ejidal* commissioner in charge of land within the *ejido*.

Not coincidentally, in 2004 these latter two individuals also held the roles of president and treasurer, respectively, of the CBT project's civil association. After only a few weeks in Ek'Balam, I felt I was quite well positioned. I had enjoyed multiple visits with local authorities who were eager to answer my questions and to agree to interviews. They were also very hospitable and considerate about introducing me to their neighbors whom I had not yet met.

It quickly became apparent, though, that my new friends and informants were only exposing me to members of a particular extended family or perhaps close friends of their family considered related through the fictive kin system created by the designation of godparents. What they had in common were positive attitudes about the CBT project and hopes that tourism would quickly lead to a new, better life. At this point I faced the question of how to gain access to the families I was not familiar with and, more important, how to identify them. The solution was a survey of the village using the transect walk method described by Setha

M. Low, Dana Taplin, and Suzanne Scheld (2005). This consisted of soliciting the help of three members of the community to guide me around the village on three separate occasions. While walking up and down each street of the village, on each occasion we worked to fill in information about the households; by listening to their descriptions of the physical layout of the village, I was able to collect information that would not otherwise have been available.

The repetition of this process with more than one member of the community increased the validity of the information gathered by ensuring that it was not simply a personal bias yielding facts about one household or another. The visual cues provided by the changing scenery prompted the guides to discuss aspects I may not have thought to include in my interview guides and questionnaires. Because of the small size of the village, the method did not use a direct line or transect. Instead, it covered all of the blocks in the town. Researchers performing Participatory Rural Appraisals (PRAs) commonly use this method. The transect walk is typically done during the initial phases of research and is used as the basis for producing a more detailed map. I conducted the transect walk at the beginning of each phase of the research.

The main information gathered through this process included genealogy, relationship to the community-based project, *ejidal* landholdings, family size and number of generations living there, main income, and presence of individuals who work outside the community. This initial stage of data collection also yielded valuable information regarding the familial groups represented in the village. Because of its small size, I was able to gather household-level data for every household in the village.

The utility of this strategy in the initial stage of fieldwork was threefold. First, by soliciting different individuals to guide me around the village, I was introduced to people from multiple social circles. The interest elicited by a resident walking with me and pausing at different houses to chat enabled me to talk with people to whom I would not otherwise have had access. Second, the information previously available with regard to the success of the community-based project came from multiple sources; however, once I was able to see the data on family structures, kin group membership, and participation in the community project, it became clear that the voices espousing the virtue of the project were those directly involved and therefore benefiting from it. The transect walk method was subsequently used in 2007, 2010, and 2012 to collect and update the census data for the village.

Historically, ethnographers have remained skeptical toward PRA and other similar field methodologies. They are often seen as "quick and dirty" approaches to understanding what ethnographers know to be very nuanced social and cultural contexts (Nyanzi et al. 2007). At the same time, ethnographic methods come with their own limitations. A combination of PRA methods, such as the

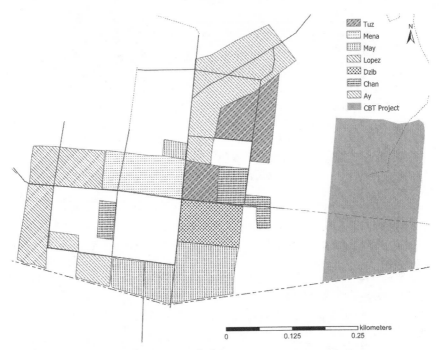

FIGURE 2.4. *Patrilocal residence patterns by kin group*

transect walk, used in conjunction with in-depth, iterative interviews proved to be the right fit in the case of this research. The use of this method in an early stage of the research made subsequent research more productive. By identifying familial ties through this systematic questioning, the kin-based social structure of the village revealed itself. The residents of Ek'Balam belong to seven extended families, or kin groups. These groups practice patrilocal residence patterns (figure 2.4) and inherit land and other resources through patriarchal descent lines.

The kin groups in Ek'Balam do not refer to themselves by the names they are assigned here, though these are all common surnames in the village. They are designated by their descent from an apical ancestor, the seven men who initially settled X'Kumil and received the *ejidal* land grant. This type of familial organization is common throughout the region and has important ramifications for agricultural production (Alexander 2006) as well as the ongoing maintenance of the community's social structure (Nutini, Carrasco, and Taggart 2009).

The history of these kin groups began at the time of the initial petition for *ejidal* land made in 1939 by five men: Claudio May Tuz, Anacleto Mena Aguilar, Delfino Ay Uc, Fulgencio Chan Chan, and Atitlano Tuz Poot. These men and their families had worked and lived on a nearby hacienda. They waited three years for their land grant to be complete, during which time two other men—Delfino Dzib Uc

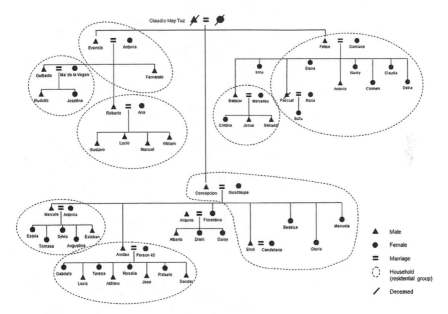

FIGURE 2.5. *May kin group*

and Miguel Lopez Pat—and their families joined the initial group. Don Delfino's family had recently left a cattle hacienda to the north, and don Miguel's family was looking for an opportunity to attain land to farm after living in Temozón.

In the May kin group diagram (figure 2.5), we see that don Claudio is the apical ancestor. The patrilocal residence pattern is also visible here. Dashed circles identify households, or residential groups—specifically, households in Ek'Balam that are part of the overall May kin group.

For example, Florentina, the daughter of Concepción and Gomercinda and granddaughter of Claudio May Tuz, is not indicated here as a household belonging to the May kin group (figure 2.6).

They reside in Ek'Balam, but Antonio and Florentina's household is primarily associated with the husband's family. Figure 2.7 is a diagram of the Mena kin group. We see here that Antonio and Florentina's family is part of the Mena kin group.

I use specific terms to refer to various levels of these structures and relationships. The term *kin group* is used in place of *extended family* because of the maintenance of consanguine familial relationships regardless of kin group membership. In the case of Florentina, she is a member of the Mena kin group. Her residence is on the north side of the town center, the opposite of the house she grew up in on the south side of the center. Her labor goes toward maintenance of the household she lives in with her husband, his parents, her children, and Antonio's brother and sister. The corn she prepares each day for her children

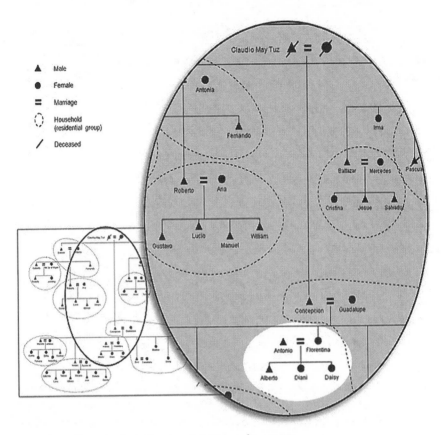

FIGURE 2.6. *Example of patrilineal organization in kin groups*

comes from her father-in-law's milpa. Kin group obligations are an important part of life in the village; however, family ties are often strong regardless of kin group membership. Concepción and Celestina May, Florentina's parents, enjoy having a large family and encourage regular gatherings at their house. On any given night, it is common to find many of Celestina's sixteen grandchildren at her home, and Florentina comes nearly every night to visit her younger sisters. When asked, she responds that she is very much a part of the May family. This is true even though her kin group is Mena.

The term *household* refers to an extended family, which consists of a nuclear family or families and their immediate relatives who share the same main residential area. The yard may contain multiple structures, but all members of a household typically share meals and pool their resources. The average household size in Ek'Balam is 6.63 persons. Each household belongs to one of the seven kin groups found in the village, and the households cluster spatially into

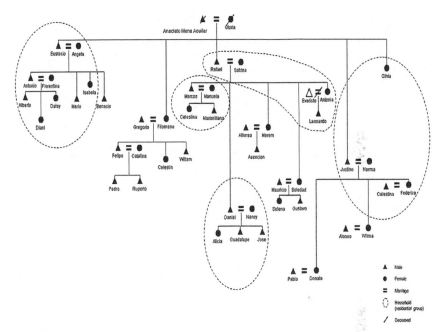

FIGURE 2.7. *Mena kin group*

groups based on patrilocal residence patterns. The rationale for delineating households from the larger kin group is that while they are linked to the larger group, they do not always have daily interactions with other members. In addition, they are autonomous with regard to participation in tourism, ecological conservation, and their domestic mode of production.

There are instances in which a daughter remains a member of her parents' kin group; though these exceptions to the rule are rare, they aid in understanding the political dynamics at play within and among the households and kin groups. The Ay kin group provides two examples of this scenario (figure 2.8). Two daughters remained in Ek'Balam with their husbands and families. They live in the Ay section of the village, and their households are part of the Ay kin group.

The Ay kin group as a whole has maintained a high level of farming and has not sold much of its land. When Antonia and Paulina married, they decided to stay in Ek'Balam. Their kin group had ample land, so their husbands were able to farm. These men are not eligible for *ejidatario* status;, however, in every other way their participation in village life is the same as that of other males.

EK'BALAM'S ARRIVAL STORY

Once I learned about the social structure and the patterns of kinship, I began to ask about the history of these families and the community. What I found was a

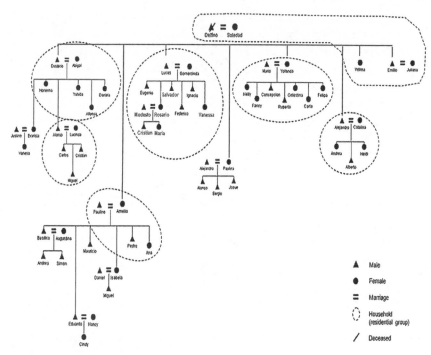

FIGURE 2.8. *Ay kin group*

much more complex history that resided in residents' notion of place. In many conversations, residents casually discussed the history of the village's founding, their fight to gain their *ejidal* land grant, and the regional and national historical contexts of these events. They presented these historical details as an important part of understanding life in the village today. History is a vital element in the narrative surrounding tourism development in Ek'Balam as well, and important historic events seem to punctuate the perception of time. Prominent among these events are references to "Los Antiguos" (the "Ancient Ones" who lived here before the Spanish came), the Caste War (1848 to 1901), and the abolition of slavery and the hacienda system (1930–40). The Caste War of Yucatán is an important piece of regional history in general and is particularly important for understanding life in and around Ek'Balam (Wells and Joseph 1996).

The first written historical references to Ek'Balam are in the "Relación de Tiquibalon" (Asensio, de Pedraza, and de Landa 1898; Hanson 2008). The conquistador Juan Gutiérrez de Picón became the *encomendero* of Tiquibalon in 1579 (Molina Solis 1896; Hanson 2008). The *encomienda* system was a tributary system in which a Maya community paid goods and service to its *encomendero*.

The Catholic Church and the *encomienda* system worked together to transform Yucatecan communities into Spanish-style municipalities consisting of individual nuclear households (Hanson 2008, 302).

Generations are categorized using events such as these that mark time. For example, among the generation of individuals born around 1950, any reference to their parents includes a phrase to locate them historically: "Well, my father and his brothers were children of some of the ones who went to the governor in Mérida to solicit land for the ejido. In this time, the campesinos were not so free. They lived in slavery, they did not have land, and they did not work for themselves." ~Don Lucio [Transcriptions 2004-0727 (1:54)].

Members of the previous generation (born around 1925) refer to their parents with stories about the Caste War to place them in history:

My deceased parents were slaves, you know, and they worked on a hacienda near here. When the war came, they helped the people hiding in the caves, the ones that ran away from the rich [hacienda owners]. They brought them a little bit of corn and some beans when they could. You should go to those caves. Some of them have carvings in the rocks where they wrote their history. When I was young and we were looking for the place to make our *ejido*, my father showed me the caves and told me these stories. ~Don Wiliam [Transcriptions 2007-0802 (42:36)]

Ek'Balam, the archaeological zone, is a Late to Terminal Classic site (AD 700–1050), although it was continuously occupied from as early as the Middle Formative (700–450 BC) and through the early Hispanic period (AD 1550–1800) (Hanson 2008). At 6 square kilometers, it is a large site center, although only about 75 percent has been excavated and restored (Houck 2004). Archaeologists only rather recently began the excavation at Ek'Balam. Most village residents have a story to tell about the process, as many of them worked with the archaeologists. Don Felipe worked during most of the initial excavation process:

At this time, the archaeological zone was covered with grass and plants, because we did not have the vision that it would become an archaeological zone. Then the people came. One person came here with us and asked if I could take him there because we were the only ones who knew much about it and the entrance was here. I told him yes, let's go. This person began to work with ten others. We helped and brought water and began to chop the jungle off the ruins. He worked there for about two weeks and left. He told everyone that Ek'Balam existed and they came to give us the good news. Then we began to care for it. ~Don Felipe [Transcriptions 2007-0718 (4:07)]

Since the excavation of the archaeological zone and the subsequent arrival of tourism, the archaeological zone has been incorporated into the historical narrative of Ek'Balam. The following account of how they selected the current village location includes an example of the incorporation of the archaeological zone into the community's history:

> When we got here, we saw the mountains of the ruins and so here we rested. There was a well here from the time of the slaves; it was a hacienda long ago. So we began to burn and chop our milpas . . . we were working and struggling. We worked in the rain and in the heat of the sun, always struggling. And now look at all we have, at how beautiful it is where we are. And the name Ek'Balam, well, those are family names that we still have here. It was always called this, and this is its history, from the ruins to the hacienda to where we are now. Other places, they don't have their history, but my history, our history is here. And why? Because of the ruins. What are the visitors going to say if they arrive and it is still abandoned? You have to have a plaza and care for the ruins. ~Don Felipe [Transcriptions 2007-0718 (26:49)]

Multiple waves of archaeologists have conducted research at the ceremonial site center (Bey, Hanson, and Ringle 1997; Vargas de la Peña, Borges, and García-Gallo 1998) and in the rural area surrounding the site (Houck 2004). Excavations of settlements dating only to the sixteenth and seventeenth centuries were conducted northeast of the site center (Hanson 2008).

For most residents of Ek'Balam, history began when they received their *ejidal* land. The second major point in their history is the move from the village where they first settled to the location of the village today. The village of Ek'Balam is located in the *ejido* of X'Kumil. This *ejido* is in the milpa zone of the Yucatán Peninsula and, until the late 1990s, was very much like the hundreds of other *ejidos* in this region. The area surrounding the archaeological zone and pueblo of Ek'Balam (figure 2.9) was occupied continuously from the Middle Formative through the Early Hispanic periods (Bey et al. 1998). The urban area covered a large space of 12 square kilometers and could have supported a population as large as 25,000.

The bulk of the research during all of the phases took place in the village of Ek'Balam, although I also conducted research with individuals in Temozón, at the archaeological site, and in neighboring *ejidal* lands. Almost all residents are descendants of the initial men who solicited and received the *ejidal* land in 1936. The site of the village was not the original settlement location and was officially founded in 1972. Because the archaeological site plays an important role in the economy and, ultimately, the identity of the village of Ek'Balam, it is included in the research setting. Proyecto Ek'Balam (the Ek'Balam Project) began in 1984, and since then the archaeological site has played an important role in the neighboring village of the same name. Between 1984 and 1994, the archaeological team employed many locals to help with the excavation and restoration processes. When the archaeological zone opened to the public in 1994, the slow

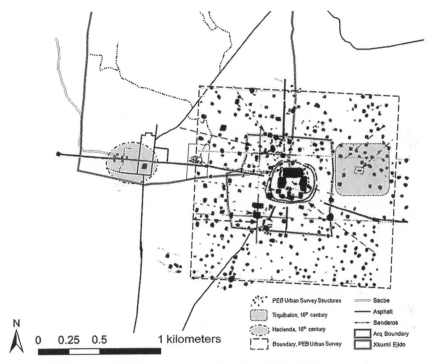

FIGURE 2.9. *Proyecto Ek'Balam urban survey (From Bey et al. 1998; Hanson 2008)*

stream of visitors began flowing. Today, residents recognize the archaeological zone as the primary attraction around which all other tourist services should be built. Archaeology and archaeological zones have been of great importance throughout the region for longer than most residents can remember, as sources of economic opportunity, history, and, more recently, heritage. In many ways this research created a variety of maps of Ek'Balam, in response to Rafael's question. Some of these are tangible products of our mapping project, such as a points of interest map for the CBT project, maps of reforestation, and maps of the archaeological zone in relationship to the village. Others are less tangible representations that shed light on exactly how the importance of the archaeological site plays out in everyday life.

Negotiating Tourism

In 1992 the five governments of the Mundo Maya, or Maya World, signed an agreement to combine their efforts in sponsoring a large-scale tourist project in the Maya regions of Mexico, Guatemala, Belize, Honduras, and El Salvador. The idea of a developed route to connect the many tourist attractions in this area was first presented by National Geographic in 1989, when it published a projected map of La Ruta Maya (Garrett 1989). The driving force behind this project was the consensus that tourist dollars were slipping away because of an uncoordinated infrastructure throughout the indigenous zones. An official map detailed the project and marked major rivers, highways, and towns assigned significance based on what they offered visitors. The map excluded towns that had little attraction for visitors to the Maya World, regardless of the fact that many of them held great importance for the Mayas of the particular area. This, then, begs the question: where are the Maya in the Maya World (Brown 1999)? How do the Maya view the marketing of their culture, and what role do they play in this process? In addition, what relationship do they have with the archaeological sites that market their heritage?

DOI: 10.5876/9781607327721.c003

In the late 1980s, residents of rural areas throughout the region were not Maya, at least not in the way many of them are today. In the 1990s, a village like Ek'Balam was not called a Pueblo Maya; while some *mestizas* were still living there and most of the men were *campesinos*, the word *Maya* was reserved mainly for the name of the language they spoke. So how can a whole population of Maya-speaking non-Mayas suddenly become Maya? This question vexes anthropologists and, as Ronald Loewe (2010, 59) points out, it comes in and out of fashion among Mesoamerican ethnographers every seventeen to twenty years, "eating everything in sight before vanishing as quickly and mysteriously as it appeared." Loewe goes on to point out that a more recent uprising of debates surrounding Maya identity was less concerned with essentialism than with the actual word *Maya*. This is likely a product of the rampant development of tourism in and around Maya-speaking communities and the complete incorporation of "Maya" as an ideological and literal destination for the Yucatán Peninsula's booming tourism trade. While scholars have been and will continue to be engaged in ongoing debates about the nature of Maya identity, the increasing importance of alternative tourism in the region is creating a role for Maya-ness in tourism marketing.

Reconstructed archaeological zones are one of the principal presentations of this cultural heritage in the region, and Ek'Balam is no exception. The reconstruction and subsequent tourism development at the nearby archaeological site prompted residents to think about the relationship of their modern village to the ancient city. In the process of creating and managing an ecosystem of authenticity, residents are in constant negotiation with both visitors and each other to determine the authentic locally and to preserve it. The contrast between the static authenticity of monuments in the ceremonial center of the archaeological zone and the dynamic authenticity of the village is stark. While questions about interpretation and accuracy surround the academic conversation about archaeological sites, they are absent from local discussions. Residents accept the facts presented by the archaeological projects. There is a certain level of disenchantment with the monuments in the archaeological zone locally, which came along with their transformation to a destination for tourists. In contrast, the hundreds of archaeological structures outside the main site retain their status as enchanted places. Spirits still guard them and are the origin of evil winds. The commodification of all things Maya has not affected the power these structures house or the way residents must treat them. The following visit with the Ay Mena family presents examples of this alternating enchantment/disenchantment.

SUMMER 2007

The quiet village is anything but this summer. When I arrived last month, people began telling me about the volunteers who would be arriving in the next few weeks. The whole town feels noticeably different since the arrival of thirty-five young people from universities throughout Mexico for the volunteer camp. This volunteer program is the latest iteration of development strategies in the village and is quite different from some of those that have come before. Previous initiatives, such as the program that funded the community-based tourism (CBT) project, consisted of capital and some capacity building but little hands-on interaction with the project. This new trend in development replaces capital with labor through a series of volunteer-led projects.

As in the village, the feeling at the Ay Mena house this summer is markedly different. Eugenio is home this weekend, but it is from work in Cancún rather than school in Temozón. He is eighteen this summer and decided to stop going to school. He started drinking while in Temozón and continued after he moved back to his mother and father's home. After only a few weeks, Lucas explained that if he was not going to study, he had to find something else to do. Goma and Lucas were thinking of helping in the milpa and finding odd jobs in Temozón, but Eugenio found there were not enough local options. He left a month ago for Cancún with his cousin Baltazar. He found work right away as a plumber's helper. His parents are disappointed but feel there is little they can do. Eugenio recognizes this but enjoys his new life and is happily sending money home to help make up for the resources his family devoted to his schooling for so many years.

His situation is increasingly typical. Each year more young men are traveling to the coast for work. This concerns some locals because one of the primary goals of the CBT project was to keep their sons and grandsons from migrating out of the community to make a living. In 2007, it seems that there are few other options. Project participation has dwindled even more since the previous summer. At the same time, the number of visitors arriving is increasing. Both of the local tourism businesses have recovered from the aftermath of the 2005 hurricane season and are thriving. For the CBT, they attribute much of the success to the volunteer programs. Individuals had come to help them translate promotional materials, paint signs, and even adjust their menu and rates to reflect similar offerings in the region.

It is late afternoon under the Almendra tree outside the blockhouse, and most of the Ay Mena family is sitting around and visiting. Sundays are days for relaxing, and even doña Goma is passing the time weaving and leaving the laundry for tomorrow. The talk around the house all afternoon has surrounded the "discovery" of an unconsolidated mound in the path of the nature trail. This summer's volunteer camp is continuing work on the nature trail project started last year, and yesterday their work landed them at the edge of a large platform. Conflating anthropologist and archaeologist, the team leader came immediately to the house to find me, thinking they had discovered a previously unknown structure. Much to their delight, it was decided that a ceremony should be held to appease the *alux* (guardian spirit, *duende* in Spanish) guarding the mound and to cleanse any evil winds that may have been released by disturbing the structure.

This morning the twenty-eight volunteers, don Marcelo, don Rafael, and I met at the site. The volunteers were walking along the trail from the Cabañas to the structure, and the three of us were coming from the village through the baseball field. On the walk there, Rafael explained the ceremony and expressed excitement at being able to perform it for the volunteers. I asked Marcelo if they would be doing this were it not for the volunteers. He replied that they would still make an offering if they disturbed a *mùul* (mound, archaeological ruin) but that it would not be very elaborate. Presumably, they would not be bringing their anthropologist and her video camera to document the event.

When we arrived, both men gasped. The sight of the twenty-eight volunteers and the numerous children they had invited visibly upset them. Children are particularly susceptible to the evil winds and should not be near monuments. I was aware of this concern but thought it was a relic from a different time. Children accompanied me to the archaeological zone on numerous occasions, and the Ay Mena family and I had visited Chichén Itzá earlier in the summer. No one had mentioned the danger this posed for the children to me before this morning. The two men scolded the children in Maya, and they quickly dispersed. It was clear to the volunteers that they should not have brought the children, and the ceremony began with a somber hush over the crowd.

Back under the Almendra tree we are all discussing the ceremony as we while away the afternoon enjoying Charritos (a popular puffed chip snack) with jalapeños and Coke. Doña Goma explains that the ruins in the archaeological zone are not the same as those found in the forest. They have been climbed, excavated, and reconstructed and are visited by hundreds of people each week. "They hardly have their guardians anymore," she explains. It seems they have become disenchanted from the residents' perspective and that the monuments themselves, much like the perception of their role as sites of heritage for modern Maya, move through phases of enchantment and disenchantment.

More than any of the other kids on this late-summer afternoon, Salvador seems enchanted with the story of the volunteers and the unexcavated mound. When they came to me to report their discovery, I showed the volunteers survey maps from articles about the archaeological zone. The maps immediately fascinated Salvador, and he has been talking about them all day. Salvador just turned fifteen last month and finished his first year of secondary school in the neighboring town of Santa Rita. He remains determined to finish what his brother Eugenio started. Salvador is acutely aware of the resources his family is working hard to provide so he can continue his education.

When the decision of whether she would continue with her studies or leave school to help with the household tasks and perfect her weaving skills came along,

Rosa quickly chose the latter. Her mother wonders why she disliked school so much and quietly wishes that she had stayed in school. Doña Gomercinda says that when she was young she had to leave school after the third grade to help with the household tasks and her younger siblings, and she laments the fact that her daughter is not taking this opportunity to complete her education. Rosa hears none of this, because when she turned fifteen she became a woman, free to make her own decisions about her education. She is now sixteen and an excellent weaver, and her hammocks augment the family income as well as allow her to begin earning her own money to buy clothes and thread for more hammocks, and this will help support her new family when she gets married. Leaving school after sixth grade is a common trend among the young women Rosa's age.

As we continue to talk about the unexcavated mounds that dot the entirety of the *ejido*, Federico and Ignacio ride up on their bikes from different directions. Federico is coming from the center of town, where he has been playing soccer with the volunteers. He will be fourteen years old in December and will graduate from sixth grade the following summer. He has begun talking about going on to secondary school so he can learn English. His cousin Baltazar continually reminds him that if he wants to work in Cancun, he should get an education so a wider variety of jobs will be open to him. A year ago, he had no time for the idea of more years in school, but spending time with the volunteers this summer seems to have changed his mind. The two boys remain each other's opposites. Ignacio rides in from having spent the morning and early afternoon pulling weeds and tending the milpa (cornfield). He is almost thirteen years old and only has two more years of school. Once he finishes sixth grade, he plans to be a *milpero* just like his father and make a living working their land.

Vanessa has been listening quietly to our conversation and focusing on her crochet project. At nine years old, she is still a bit small to weave a full-sized hammock, but she wants very much to have projects to work on this summer like her mother and older sister. Doña Goma is teaching her to crochet, and she is engrossed in the task. When she is not working on her crocheting, she is in the town center visiting with the volunteers or the missionary group that has started to frequent the village this summer.

The presence of so many outside groups in the village creates a number of new conversations about what exactly it is that attracts visitors. Residents are beginning to be accustomed to tourists visiting, and they attribute this to interest in ancient Maya culture. What they are uncertain of is what exactly attracts the different types of visitors who say they are not here to be tourists, such as volunteers and missionaries. Eugenio tells us that it is similar to what he sees in Cancún. He reports that every day, busloads of people come to volunteer and do projects in local communities. It is progress, he says, development. These are different from the projects the government brings to the villages, though. With the volunteer tourists, they get to do something to help and then be tourists as well.

TOURISM IN THE MAYA WORLD

While the arrival of visitors is a recent development in Ek'Balam, it is nothing new in the Maya World more broadly. The Maya are perhaps the most heavily studied culture group in the world. The Maya World spans the nation-states of Mexico, Belize, Guatemala, El Salvador, and Honduras. This spatial classification is part of the larger culture area of Mesoamerica, which stretches from central Mexico to Costa Rica. Paul Kirchhoff (1943) first defined Mesoamerica as both a place of study and an object of study using the designation of cultural traits found throughout the region. From an archaeological point of view, these traits are reliance on maize, beans, and squash as domesticated crops; religious practices involving monumental architecture; a polytheistic belief system; use of a ritual calendar, and market exchange as the basis of the economic system (Smith and Masson 2000). While these are shared cultural traits, they are not necessarily unifying. By the 1980s, archaeologists had replaced the traits with practices (Hendon and Joyce 2004) and employed the model of Mesoamerica as a fragmented area of diverse cultures connected through trade. Ethnographers first defined Mesoamerica based on the cultural traits they observed in the communities where they worked. Many of these traits had to do with the common style of dress and economic means of production (Tax and Redfield 1968). While Kirchhoff's southern boundary of Mesoamerica was just east of Guatemala and the western tip of Honduras, some argue that it should actually extend further south and east through Central America (Fox et al. 1981; Lange 1976). Language is another factor used to define Mesoamerica as stretching from northern Mexico south to the Gulf of Nicoya in Costa Rica (Creamer 1987).

Since the beginning of the tourist era in the 1970s, the Maya areas experiencing rapid tourism development have been increasingly shifting from a subsistence lifestyle to reliance on wage labor and handicraft production for the tourism industry. These new means of production are seen in villages in the highlands of Guatemala (Annis 1987) as well as in urban centers (Little 2004b) and in Chiapas (Earle and Simonelli 2005). The Yucatán Peninsula is developing at rates far and above those seen in other parts of the Maya World (Torres and Momsen 2005). Scholars working in this area find that loss of land and the marketing of both the physical and human environments have led to inflation and displacement of traditional local industries (Juárez 2002; Kintz 1990; Pi-Sunyer, Thomas, and Daltabuit 2001). Often, the only potential for the Maya in the tourist industry is the occupation of bottom-level positions, pushing them even further toward the periphery and transforming them into what some have called "a rural proletariat" (Re Cruz 1996). When examining the current position of the Maya in these areas, it is necessary to remember that in some respects their subordinate status has changed very little since colonial times (Farriss 1984; Clendinnen 2003). At the same time Mayas are pushed out of some means of participation in tourism throughout the region, commodified Maya-ness is a major component of the attraction of millions of tourists to destinations in the Maya World. The question remains then, what is Maya?

The development of Cancún, like most tourism development, occurred in many phases. It began as a government economic policy favoring international and national economic investment in the hotel industry. During this process, the Mexican state took on the new role of initiating and planning tourism development (Clancy 2001b). From the conception of the idea to the receipt of $21.5 million in funding from the Inter-American Development Bank (IDB) in 1971, the "Cancun Project" was orchestrated by the government through newly formed and empowered agencies such as FONATUR (Fondo Nacional de Fomento al Turismo) and the National Foundation for the Stimulation of Tourism.

While the development of Cancún brought millions of people to the region in the 1970s, these eager tourists were hardly the first foreigners to explore Yucatán. Perhaps the most prominent of the early explorers in Mesoamerica was John Lloyd Stephens, who was accompanied by Frederick Catherwood in his expeditions through Central America, Chiapas, and Yucatán (Evans 2004). After they returned from their first expedition in Central America, Stephens published a monograph filled with tales of adventure and incredible sketches. The success of this first publication (Stephens 1841) funded the duo's second expedition to Yucatán. The archaeological travel narratives that resulted from the second trip were published as a monograph in 1843, to great success (Stephens 1843). Perhaps the excitement over Stephens's stories from Central America, Chiapas, and Yucatán stems from their singular tone and approach to documentation. Stephens was not interested in postulating grand new theories about the origin of the monuments he found or in rehashing the "dubious scholarship" of the earlier generation of European explorers in the region (Evans 2004; Black 1990). Instead, he set out to quietly propose that the ruins of Maya civilization were not of Old World origin but in fact were created indigenously and at a much later date than was previously argued (Evans 2004, 45).

One of the themes that runs through Stephens's writings is the contrast of the glorious civilization glimpsed by the public in Catherwood's drawings and the ruin in which the people around the crumbling monuments lived. Examples of this juxtaposition are seen in Catherwood's drawings that position scantily clad, dark-skinned people amid the ruined structures. This imagery reminds readers that the people left here are not the great architects of these cities but instead are merely porters and laborers (Evans 2004, 66). This sentiment carried over into early ethnographic work in the region as well. According to Redfield, the relationship between the ancient and modern Maya was artificial and the product of anthropological imagination: "The Maya Indians of present-day Yucatán can be said to dwell in the ruined house of their ancestors . . . but it is the archaeologist, not the Indian, who sees the grandson living in the broken shell of the grandfather's mansion; certainly the Indian attributes to the situations no quality of pathos. The ruins are not, for him, a heritage" (Redfield 1932, 152). During this period, ancient history and historical remains were the destinations; however, they had no connection to modern Maya residents. People living near abandoned cities were a labor pool. At this point, history was not heritage.

In many ways, the incorporation of Maya heritage in the development and promotion of Cancún is similar to the way early explorers and archaeologists relied on the Maya. That is, the residents, or modern Maya, were a labor pool. The history of the ancient Maya was promoted as an attraction, and little connection was made between the two. While archaeological remains had then become both patrimony of the nation and a destination, they were still, for the modern Maya, not a heritage.

TOURISM AS DEVELOPMENT

Mexico has a long relationship with tourism, and the government has seen this as a vehicle of economic development since the early part of the twentieth century, when the country emerged from the Mexican Revolution. The debate over how to cater to the demands of the tourism industry and maintain Mexico's unique national identity began as early as the 19302 (Berger and Wood 2010). In the 1990s, some tourists began looking for an alternative to the sterile, constructed experience offered by the resorts of Cancún and the Maya Riviera. Travelers who saw themselves as adventurers rather than tourists were searching for unique experiences and felt that finding something off the beaten path would provide this for them. The Yucatán Peninsula, once Mexico's Wild West, was now tamed. As Nicholas Dagen Bloom (2006, 8) notes, "The sharp edges of the Mexican experience have gradually been rubbed off, leaving behind a pleasing essence of foreign travel." This was in many ways the ultimate marker of success for the Cancun Project and was one of the most attractive factors for many visitors. Others, however, felt that authentic Maya culture was the only culture left in the region. Many modern Maya communities are off the beaten path, both literally and figuratively. Even those who do live along major tourism routes present a lifestyle that is exotic to visitors. Mass tourism development led the bushwhacking campaign, and now the Maya Riviera is, in the eyes of many tourists, "beaten."

This marked a major shift in the aesthetic of touring in Yucatán. Now, modern Maya were sought out as both attraction and destination. By the mid-1990s the state secretary of tourism, the National Commission for the Development of

Indigenous Villages (CDI), and the Comisión Nacional Forestal (National Forestry Commission, CONAFOR) were identifying villages to target for community-based tourism and conservation initiatives. Cultural tours that incorporated authentic living Maya culture, archaeological sites, and eco-tourism activities became wildly popular. The past finally became, for the Maya, a heritage.

From a community development perspective, eco-tourism presents an unexpected opportunity to improve communities and standards of living (Belsky 1999). State sponsorship of eco-tourism and other alternative tourism projects in Mexico began in 1989, when the Instituto Nacional Indigena (National Indigenist Institute, INI) implemented the project Indigenous Communities, Ecology, and Production for Sustainable Development (Pueblos Indigenas, Ecologica y Produccion para el Desarrollo Sustenable) (Palomino and López Pardo 2012). The goal was to develop culturally appropriate and ecologically sustainable projects, and in 1989 they supported the creation of eight indigenous eco-tourism projects (Palomino and López Pardo 2007). By the late 1990s the tourism industry was experiencing an increasing demand for "conserved destinations and living culture" (Palomino and López Pardo 2012, 993). This was the catalyst needed for INI to reorganize the agency as the Comisión Nacional para el Desarrollo de los Pueblos Indígenos (National Commission for the Development of Indigenous Villages, CDI) in 2000 to fortify government support of eco-tourism projects. Between 2001 and 2005, CDI spent 119.8 million pesos (US$10.9 million) on the creation of 246 projects. These projects involved 39,742 indigenous people in 23 states across the country (Gasca Zamora et al. 2010). One of the earliest projects was the CBT project in Ek'Balam, which received initial funding in 2001.

The difference between the strategies employed by the state and the tactics used by residents is clear in the interactions that surround the development of tourism in Ek'Balam and other, similar destinations (De Certeau 2004). The state sponsors and markets Maya-ness as a strategy for soliciting tourism, and residents determine just how they will enact this marketing tool at the local level. These goals are communicated to villages through agencies such as INDEMAYA (Instituto para el Desarrolla de la Cultura Maya del Estado de Yucatán [Institute for the Development of the Maya Culture of the Yucatán State]) in 2001 and the CDI in 2003. The CDI's mission and vision are to "guide, coordinate, promote, support, monitor, and evaluate programs, projects, strategies and actions to reach the public and sustainable development and full exercise of the rights of indigenous peoples and communities in accordance with Article 2 of the Constitution of the United Mexican States" (CDI 2003).

While agencies such as the CDI and INDEMAYA are state agencies, they work to create local or grassroots support through their emphasis on community-based development initiatives, affording them an image of being hands-off. This complements the regional sentiment of separation from the national government characteristic of Yucatán.

The village of Ek'Balam is an example of a community that has been targeted for the development of alternative tourism initiatives. The lack of education available to descendant communities regarding their Maya heritage is but one example of disconnects between the touristic presentation of Maya culture and heritage and the actual practice of exploring that culture. The designation of history as heritage is the crucial component in the creation and maintenance of an ecosystem of authenticity.

The relationship between host and guest has been characterized in myriad ways since the late 1970s, when scholars began examining tourism. Some have presented it as an unequal relationship based on wealth disparities, and others have spent much time looking for the "impact" of the host on the guest. Since the shift in many of our field sites to alternative tourism development strategies, we have seen subtle changes in the paradigms researchers use to frame their work. Regardless of whether it functions well, the community-based tourism model at least forces us to consider the agency of the hosts as developers and managers of tourism destinations. Numerous case studies report on the way tourism affects the lives of local populations; however, Amanda Stronza (2001, 263) states that "we have yet to develop models or analytical frameworks that could help us predict the conditions under which locals experience tourism in particular ways." This is especially true when investigating alternative forms of tourism, such as eco-tourism and community-based tourism initiatives.

These nuanced differences between types of travel excursions and motivations necessitate a brief discussion of the typologies of tourism. Both volunteer and solidarity tourism fall into the category of alternative tourism, along with eco-tourism and other types of experiences that emphasize meaningful cultural exchange and avoidance of the so-called beaten path (Jafari 1987; Weaver 2010). Raymond Noronha defines "institutionalized" tourists as those who use packaged tours organized by agencies and do not step out of their Western ideals of comfort. This causes the need for facilities and services to which these tourists will be accustomed, and, in the author's view, it "becomes the turning point where [hosts] lose social, political, and economic control over tourism development" (Noronha 1976).

Alternative tourism arose alongside alternative development theory, which is a critique of the modernization theory that preceded it. This paradigm entered the development discourse because of increasing dissatisfaction with previous models that were based on the successful examples of developed countries and attempted to implement projects without regard for local conditions. Out of alternative development theory came the basic needs approach and participatory strategies such as Participatory Action Research (PAR) and Participatory Rural Appraisal

(PRA) (Greenwood, Whyte, and Harkavy 1993; Chambers 1994). Many tourism researchers claim that this paradigm has the most relevance to the study and planning of tourism development (Brohman 1996; Sharpley 2000; Telfer and Wall 1996) because of its emphasis on sustainability concepts; however, it is difficult to define the paradigm in the same way sustainable tourism can be defined. Some of the strategies employed in alternative tourism destinations mirror those found in alternative development initiatives (Reid 2003; Saarinen 2006). Alternative tourism denotes a type of tourism that is developed in a different way. Community-based tourism, indigenous tourism, and other small-scale sustainable tourism endeavors are examples of alternative tourism. David Weaver states that Thomas Hinch and Richard Butler provide a good definition of indigenous tourism to help clarify these concepts (Weaver 2010). They define it as "tourism activity in which indigenous people are directly involved either through control and/or by having their culture serve as the essence of attraction" (Hinch and Butler 2007, 9).

Tourism is often hailed as a vehicle to development and, since the 1990s, as a strategy that can yield high levels of sustainability (Ashley and Maxwell 2001). Until recently, most literature did not question this common association between the terms *tourism* and *development* as separate ideas sharing an intimate causal relationship (i.e., tourism equals development). Perhaps the similar evolution of tourism planning frameworks and development theory negated the need for a conceptual bridge between tourism and development studies. Various authors are beginning to question this relationship (Sharpley and Telfer 2002; Simms 2007). Examples are Richard Sharpley's (2000) examination of the theoretical divide between development and tourism and Donald G. Reid's (2003) discussion of the relationship between tourism and globalization. Sharpley questions whether tourism development can actually be placed under the purview of sustainable development and suggests that it may be "a red herring [that] draws attention away from many of the realities of tourism development, realities which are in opposition to a number of the principles and objectives embodied in the concept of sustainable development" (Sharpley 2000, 14). He provides a theoretical framework to link sustainable tourism to sustainable development principles, something that until recently was missing from the literature. To understand the relationship between tourism and alternative development theory, it is important to review the evolution of development paradigms and trace it through some major shifts in both practice and theory. As Anja Simms (2007, 4) cautions, any brief review of development theory risks oversimplifying this ambiguous and often poorly defined concept; yet a solid theoretical base through which today's development thought can be understood with regard to tourism development is of great importance.

The relationship between tourism and sustainability is fragile at best. Some go so far as to suggest that sustainable tourism cannot be accomplished vis-à-vis the concept of sustainable development because the production and consumption aspects of the tourism industry are potentially incompatible with the principles of sustainable or alternative development theory (Arroyo et al. 2013; Buckley 2012; Jackson 1997). Sharpley (2000) argues that this inconsistency positions tourism development more suitably in the realm of modernization theory. Others question that argument and, in turn, suggest that while sustainable tourism is not always sustainable development, it can be a means to that end (Cromwell et al. 2001; Wearing and McDonald 2002).

Participatory development has recently come into the favor of many major international donors because of their dissatisfaction with the outcomes and effectiveness of aid programs designed following the traditional development model (Abraham and Platteau 2004). For the individual programs, this means the participation of the intended beneficiaries is critical to the project's success because of the recognition of the importance of their cultural knowledge. This approach has been called for throughout the last two decades but was slow to be implemented into the scope of international development (Cornwall 2008; Li 2006). One of the major components of this shift is the realization that many development programs have repeatedly resulted in failure. These programs did not succeed largely because they were poorly designed and failed to consider socio-cultural factors (Cernea 1991). Michael Cernea terms the application of social knowledge in development as "putting people first." He argues that this is "not just a goodwill appeal to the humanitarian feelings of project planners" but an integral factor in the effectiveness of these programs (Cernea 1991, 7).

Attempts at defining participation within the developmental context are as varied and unsuccessful as the attempts at defining community previously discussed. Some say it is the inclusion of local knowledge in the project design and implementation; others such as Ghazala Mansuri and Vijayendra Rao (2004) counter that labeling a project "participatory" is often a planning-level construct that ultimately does not consider local knowledge. Robert McTaggart offers a useful alternative in his definition of participation through its distinction from involvement. He sees authentic participation as a situation in which participants share in the conceptualization, practice, and implementation of research (McTaggart 1997), whereas involvement simply refers to the amorphous local knowledge project model criticized by Mansuri and Rao (2004). This level of collaboration results in what Duncan MacLean Earle and Jean M. Simonelli (2005, 140) call the "fast-food model of community involvement with its own development decisions."

The participatory approach can be a challenge in the context of sustainable development of tourism because of its emphasis on "the community." Jarkko Saarinen (2006) notes that the host community is made up of different groups with different ideas as to the manner in which tourism should be developed, and the question of which group is defining the parameters of the community is troublesome. In addition, sustainability should not be mistaken for a vehicle to equality among members of the host community and other participants in the tourism industry (Saarinen 2006, 1123). This critique notwithstanding, participatory development and its "community" approach have great potential for improving rural development, especially as it pertains to tourism. The cultural commoditization and performance aspects of tourism require a strategy for distributing benefits that is born out of some level of consensus among members of the community in question. Once this is accounted for, the level of sustainability maintained by a project will undoubtedly increase because of the increased incentive for involvement of local stakeholders and community members (Aas, Ladkin, and Fletcher 2005). Various recommendations for proceeding in this direction with future tourism development have been suggested by Susan C. Stonich and other social scientists (Stonich 2005; Carr, Ruhanen, and Whitford 2016; Dinica 2009).

EK'BALAM, PUEBLO MAYA

Change and continuity are common themes in Ek'Balam when the topic of tourism arises. Many people discuss the economic changes households are undergoing, while others talk about the things in the village that should remain the same. There is a push for maintaining a level of authenticity in Ek'Balam. Some residents link the changes in the village directly to the arrival of tourism in the region, such as the effect of young people traveling to Cancún for work. Don Felipe explained:

> In reality, ourselves as Mayas . . . it is a shame to see that in other places our traditions have gone into the past, when we were the owners, the originals. We should continue conserving our past for our children so that in their time, it will not be lost—our customs and traditions are the most essential to our life. Our people are beginning to see what has changed. The people of before dressed like this normally, in the Yucatecan way with their white shirt and pants and their little sandals like these and their little hat. But today very few of us use these sandals. It embarrasses them to wear these sandals. We are not now like the people from many years ago. Our ancestors, our grandparents, they wore clothes like this, but today the men, our sons, do not want to put this on. ~Don Felipe [Transcriptions 2004-0729]

There was a "Disney-esque" feeling to this conversation. Sitting in the yard of a new blockhouse with a man who had previously lived in Cancún for fifteen years and now runs the taxi service in Ek'Balam filled me with the sense that tourism has made these vanishing traditions profitable. Would he or anyone there be expounding the value of conserving these old ways if they could not be marketed as touristic performance? When defining authenticity, how far back should the village reach?

The way residents design and maintain authenticity is a subject of constant debate. Prior to 2005, some households chose the more modern and expensive blockhouses over the traditional thatch houses found in the village; however, these were very expensive. The construction of a blockhouse was a display of wealth. In 2005 the Comisión Nacional de Vivienda (National Housing Commission, CONAVI) program brought blockhouses to nearly every lot in the village to help rebuild after Hurricane Wilma. The result is that while most lots still have at least one thatch structure, almost all of them have a blockhouse. There are advantages and disadvantages to the new style of construction. While the houses are extremely hot in the summer months, they help keep out the cold, wet night air in the winter. There is a consensus that they are the nicer option, and many families prefer the blockhouse over a thatch house as the primary living area.

From the outside, the houses have changed the appearance of the village. This is undesirable according to some residents, including the leaders of the Cabañas. To combat the modernization of Ek'Balam, the leaders tasked some volunteers with creating an urban plan that would restore the village's authentic look. One of the volunteers created a mockup of the plan as part of the summer camp program in 2012. The highlights of the plan are a proposal to create a thatch awning in front of every blockhouse and to construct a ball court in the center of town.

Into this discussion of an ecosystem of authenticity, tourism development, and indigeneity comes capital. Capital is, in one form or another, the ultimate goal of a successful development endeavor. The role of economic capital in this case is clear: tourists bring money. They have to pay to stay at the Cabañas, and they may pay a local taxi to shuttle them back and forth to the archaeological zone on a particularly hot day. If they are staying at the Cabañas they have to buy their meals there, and—perhaps most significant—they purchase hammocks and other handicrafts from women around the village. Because the CBT project dictates that access to participation relies on *ejidatario* status, land and land tenure are the contexts for examining economic capital. The role of land in Ek'Balam is much more than economic in nature, which makes it an interesting object of focus. It is both economic capital and cultural capital. Access to land through an individual's status as an *ejidatario* is what provides his household with the cultural capital to benefit from tourism through the Cabañas project. Further, the *ejidal* system serves as a mechanism for social regulation by which the traditional practice of community labor can be controlled (Castellanos 2010b).

Pierre L. Bourdieu (1986) was the first to discuss the concept in his essay "The Forms of Capital." What is unique about the context of tourism development in Ek'Balam is that economic, or material, capital is directly generated by and reliant on cultural capital. Bourdieu (1986, 243) states that "in an undifferentiated society, in which access to the means of appropriating the cultural heritage is equally distributed, embodied culture does not function as cultural capital." In Ek'Balam, appropriation of cultural heritage is anything but equally distributed. In the case of Ek'Balam, embodied culture is cultural capital. Residents gain this form of capital over time as negotiations with tourists become impressed on the individual's habitus. There is an explicitly performative aspect to this process, as discussed shortly. This, according to Bourdieu, is the product of frequent negotiations that over time have taught people what it is that tourists expect. Chapter 6 explores cultural capital and argues that residents maintain access to it through specific tactics and strategies.

A household's level of symbolic capital determines access to tourists and therefore the opportunity for the sale of handicrafts and the presentation of cultural capital. Bourdieu (1986, 27) defines symbolic capital as "capital—in whatever form—in so far as it is represented . . . as a socially constituted cognitive capacity." Examples of symbolic capital in Ek'Balam are access to the formal role of cook or housekeeper at the community-based tourism project and purveyor of sodas and snacks through an informal commercial endeavor. Members of a household gain access to the formal role by having as a member an *ejidatario* who is participating in the community-based tourism project. In this case, access to symbolic capital is the key component to gaining cultural capital and material capital. In the case of the informal role, however, the political ecology of the household and its land-use decisions generate symbolic capital.

The last form of capital at work in Ek'Balam is social capital, which refers to the quantitative and qualitative nature of social relations. This is called a link between the theoretical benefits of participation and the actual success of the community-based approach but is also roundly criticized as an un-measurable value that is about as tangible and useful as the unquestioned ideals of "community" or "participation" (Fine 2001). The criticisms of social capital as applied to development notwithstanding, it is a useful concept in this case because it deals with the meaning of membership at the group and individual levels. The prime example of this is the relationship between *ejidal* membership and benefit from the community-based tourism project. Social capital is also at work in relations between hosts and guests (Jones 2005). Residents' ability to interact with non-locals—be they tourists, volunteers, or funders—is dependent on their social capital and allows them to generate additional capital.

I have spoken at length with each of the last five municipal commissioners, and they all have explained that Ek'Balam is now a Pueblo Maya. What remains unclear is what this actually means to them. What does it mean to the general population? Further, how is a household's decision as to whether to participate in tourism a factor in the meaning it gives to the village's status as a Pueblo Maya? The reason I ask these questions is that "Ek'Balam has something special going for it," as Joan, the proprietor of Hotel Eden, would say. Joan was the first foreigner to start a business in the village, and she has seen many changes in her ten years there. She periodically wonders aloud at the sheer volume of people coming from great distances to do something they see as helpful for the community. "Why Ek'Balam?" she often asks me, thinking I may have an anthropological theory that could help explain this phenomenon. If we were to ask one of the local politicians, they would say it is precisely because it is a Maya village. It is a Pueblo Maya.

The use of identity as a strategy for attracting tourism and, perhaps more important, external aid and development initiatives is nothing new. Similarly, the performance of this leveraged identity for economic gain from tourism is not a novel occurrence. What are of interest are the daily choices residents made since the archaeological zone opened in 1994 that have shaped the development of tourism in their community. These choices include negotiations with federal funding agencies, regional non-governmental organizations, foreign and national entrepreneurs, tourists, volunteers, and each other. The latter category of negotiations deserves the most attention because this is what happens daily, and the results of these negotiations determine how a household will engage with external actors. Residents conduct these negotiations over the cooking fire, in the fields, and on the way to grind the day's corn.

The negotiators are members of this community only as far as it is geographically bound. That is, they all live within the 17 square hectares, or 42.01 acres, defined as the urban area of Ek'Balam. Beyond that, the utility of the term *community* as a defining factor wanes. What is more useful in understanding the intra-community relations are kin groups and households. The use of community as a definitive category is common throughout ethnographic work and particularly stands out in Mesoamerica's ethnological record as the most prevalent unit of analysis from the 1930s through the 1970s. The early organization of rural dwellers throughout the Mesoamerican countryside may have spurred this. Many development programs conceive of the community as a framework for and object of development, as I discuss in later chapters. For the purpose of this study, I limit the use of community to references to the community-based tourism project and instead refer to residents, households, and families made up of extended kin groups.

Recent literature on tourism has called for a change in the way we present research. Many previous studies have focused on the impact of tourism on a local population. This study avoids employing "impact" as a framework for understanding tourism in Ek'Balam to the greatest extent possible; however, because something like agency is difficult—if not impossible—to quantify, we must recognize that while residents are autonomous actors working within a politicized system (Stronza 2001), they are also beholden to the factors that are out of their control. They happen, for instance, to speak Yucatec Maya and to live 300 meters from the archaeological site of Ek'Balam.

Land Tenure, Tourism, and Free Trade

The role of land reform in Mexico's post-Revolutionary era has had an immense influence on the social, economic, and political environments in today's agrarian communities. While the economic implications of land and land tenure in Maya communities in Yucatán are readily apparent, the social and political importance of land is sometimes understated. Mexico's *ejidal* system consists of property rights and land tenure, which play a role that is much more than economic in nature (Haenn 2005; Klepeis and Vance 2003; Perramond 2008). The possession of land and the status of *ejidatario* (member of an *ejido*) are important factors in social relationships both within the community and between individuals and kin groups. The status of an *ejidatario* gives social power and influence to both the individual and the person's household (Castellanos 2010b). In addition, the view of *ejidatarios* as descendants of those who fought the hacienda owners in the Mexican Revolution affords them a higher status. Because an understanding of land tenure requires it to be regionally and historically contextualized and embedded in the national political economy, this chapter discusses the outcomes of the struggle for land during the Mexican Revolution (1910–20) and

DOI: 10.5876/9781607327721.c004

the eventual land reform and appropriation that finally came to Yucatán and Chiapas in the 1930s (Fallaw 2001).

This chapter outlines some major changes in the country's land tenure system, and this visit with the Ay Mena family (January 2008) presents some opinions about what people should and should not do with their land. The community-based tourism (CBT) project in this case was overlaid on the existing *ejidal* system. Given that this is a communal system for land use, the assumption was that the same structure would be perfect for building a project like the Cabañas that could be shared among all. The flaw in this logic is that not everyone in the village lives in a household associated with a member of the communal land group—an *ejidatario*. Because of this, the development of the project was contentious and received little support from community members who were not able to be directly involved or to benefit from its potential. The tensions that arose during the project planning and implementation phases, however, did not develop because of this project. Instead, they were iterations of tensions among families, households, and kin groups in the community that date back to the earliest days of the town.

WINTER 2008

It is incredibly cold on this January night, and everyone is staying close to the fire. Eugenio is home, although shortly he will head out into the night to visit with friends and drink as many beers as he can keep hidden from his mother and father when he comes in to sleep. This is an increasingly common pastime among the younger generation. No stores in the village sell alcohol, however, so there is a common assumption among many families that living in Temozón increases the likelihood of young men learning to drink. It has been about a year and a half since 'Genio left home for the coast, and this leaves his mother quite worried. He realizes this but sees migration as the only viable option for him. He is not interested in farming, does not want to participate in the CBT project, and wants to earn money for his family.

The other children are excited when he is home and try to be as close to him as possible without annoying their big brother, who now lives such a different life than they do. Everyone is interested in his life there, though only one—Federico—shows interest in going there himself when he is older. The children are young though, and this feeling may change when it comes time for them to seek their own lives. Doña Gomercinda is aware of this and will worry about them when the time comes, as she now worries about Eugenio. As she says, you never know if he is healthy or sick, working or walking the streets. Cancún is a common option for young men in the village, and each year more and more are heading to the coast to find work as masons, carpenters, and day laborers. This trend has multiple effects on the village. Some continue living in two places, with one foot in their traditional world and the other in the very fast-paced modern world of Cancún, while others make a complete move with their wives and children and return to their villages only occasionally.

The younger boys provide a dramatic contrast to Eugenio's demeanor and his parents' concerns. Federico and Nacho are gleeful in the first days after school has ended for the winter break. Both boys are eager to graduate from the sixth grade: Nacho so he can work in the fields with his father and Fede so he can start working on the coast with his brother and cousins. For now, Fede has to be content with working in the fields during the school break. They rise early to eat a few tortillas and then ride their bikes out to the milpa and return in the early afternoon full of energy and stories about their morning. When asked if they ever consider going on to study like their two older brothers have, Nacho is especially quick to explain that his brothers did not want to work in the fields under the sun, and he does not want to read books and study hard. "I will follow my father even if my brother does not," he proclaims proudly and adamantly.

Lucas is talking with 'Genio and the other boys tonight about an offer they received to purchase a piece of their land. A church group is looking for a parcel of land in the village on which to construct a small church and provide lodging for visiting missionaries. One of the group's representatives has become close to the Ay Mena family in the few years since they began visiting the village, largely because of Vanessa's interest in them. He has asked Lucas and Goma if they would consider selling the church a small corner of their large lot. Lucas declined, but it brought up the topic of how they would divide their land eventually. Eugenio is twenty now, and his parents are beginning to ask him when he will get married and come back home. Goma says that even if he finds a girl on the coast who is not accustomed to rural life, she will take on their washing and cooking until she learns how to do it herself. In short, Goma will be fifty next year and is ready to be a grandmother.

Salvador breaks into the conversation to share his opinion about the sale of land. He is adamant that this land is an inheritance from his grandfather and that he does not want the family to sell it to a gringo missionary. At seventeen, Salvador is in ninth grade. He will graduate from secondary school in July and go on to high school in September. He is following in the path of his older brother, though he says he will not start drinking and will finish school. Salvador is curious about the world around him and loves to go to the archaeological zone. He takes any opportunity he can find to travel outside the village. Just last month he ran with the Virgin of Guadalupe runners from Chiapas to Yucatán. Salvador is also very family-oriented. His dream is to find a job that is interesting, that will keep him learning, and that will let him stay in Ek'Balam.

The theme of discovery seems to characterize much of the winter this year. It took a great amount of pleading and convincing on the part of Nacho, Federico, and their cousins, but don Lucas finally agreed to organize an expedition to the old village site of X'Kumil. No one has been there since they left in 1970, and the men leading the expedition talked at length about how they would be able to locate it.

This winter I am working on a mapping project that has ballooned into something much larger than I had imagined. Initially, the plan was to create a map for the village that included various points of interest visitors may like to know more about. Once I began to work with various community members, however, it became clear that there were a number of opinions about what to include on a map of Ek'Balam. Some of the young men in town got the idea that we needed to include the old village site on the map. "You have the Hacienda Kantó and the place where we are now, but you're missing the part in between," Nacho exclaimed when I showed him a working draft of the map. While I thought we were looking at a spatial representation, he was concerned about the temporal nature of the map and the fact that a period of around forty years was missing from it.

Our expedition set out on a hot, clear morning. Sixteen residents of varying ages and I piled into the back of the pickup truck belonging to the CBT project and headed out to find X'Kumil. We were able to make it most of the way in by car, but the forest became too thick for us to continue. We walked the last mile or so into the village site. As we progressed through the trees, they became larger and larger. At one point, Federico remarked that he had never seen trees so old. Goma did not come along. She decided it was best to leave the space to the young people who were eager to learn about the hometown of their fathers and grandfathers.

Back in the kitchen that evening, we are taking turns sitting close to the fire. We hear laughter and see the boys, Fede and Nacho, stow their bikes after riding around town. It is too cold to be outside, and Goma happily invites them to warm themselves in the kitchen. She tells Rosa to heat some water for hot chocolate so we can all stay warm. The temperature has dipped to 61°F. This does not seem as though it should feel so cold, particularly for me who left winter behind in upstate New York. The open construction of the houses, so perfectly adapted to summer heat and humidity, does little to keep out winter's chilly gusts and damp air.

Maria del Rosario is eighteen now and is kept busy around the house. She has started working at Joan's Hotel Eden in the kitchen and around the hotel cleaning rooms and doing laundry. She has a quiet, stoic character, and her family is surprised that she enjoys working with Joan and her guests. As the eldest daughter, Rosa has been responsible for helping with cooking and housework since she was quite young. She enjoys the chance to be around other people. While she does not particularly care for interaction with the visitors, she likes having a reason to get out of the house. The money she makes helps with the family's expenses and allows for the extra amount needed to keep Salvador in school.

Federico and Nacho are back to talking about the missionaries in town and the rising land sales. Federico thinks it is exciting to meet new people as they come into town and bring their guests. Nacho feels gringos should not be allowed to own land and forested areas that belong to the community. He does not like to participate in any of the missionary's activities and shares Salvador's adamancy that their land is not for sale. He begins regaling us with a story about the children of one of the local families that has sold most of its land. Marcos, a member of that family, always wanted to farm, just like his father. Their family's parcel was adjacent to the Ay Menas' parcel. He and Nacho would spend days in the forest and fields, setting traps for birds, clearing the trails, and learning about the land that would eventually be theirs to work. Marcos's family sold the last piece of their parcel to a woman who is developing a yoga retreat for tourists. This was a year ago, and since then both of Marcos's older brothers have had to leave town to look for work on the coast. Marcos is twelve, the same age as Nacho, but he now knows he will not have land waiting for him to work when he finishes the sixth grade in two years. For Nacho, whose plan is to finish primary school as quickly as possible so he can dedicate all of his time to working his land, this is a tragic and cautionary tale.

Federico, in contrast, is heeding his cousin's counsel and beginning to think about school. For the first time, he has mentioned that he might want to keep studying after he finishes sixth grade next summer. His interests are moving away from farming the more he learns about 'Genio's life in Cancún. For him, a life of adventure on the coast is beginning to be more appealing than farming in the village. Vanessa is eleven and is beginning to think she might continue her schooling. Last summer she spent quite a lot of time with the volunteers, making set appointments to play with them in her characteristic way. Tonight she is helping Goma pull down extra blankets for everyone while Rosa passes around gourds filled with hot chocolate and Lucas stokes the fire. It will be another cold night for sleeping. While the children complain about the cold, Goma has confided to me that she likes nights such as this because they keep everyone close together. As her family grows and the boys start making plans for their own lives, she cherishes these moments when all six of her children are content to sip hot chocolate and stay close to the fire and to each other.

AGRARIAN REFORM

The lands distributed to the indigenous groups after the Mexican Revolution were agricultural communities called *ejidos*. Eyler N. Simpson (1937, xiii) defined *ejido* as "the word used to refer to all types of land which have been restored to agricultural communities under the land reform process. By extension the word is also used to designate the communities possessing such lands." Individual residents, or *ejidatarios*, received plots of land that would remain in their families for generations, though not as private property (Gonzales 2002).

It was not until the presidency of Lázaro Cárdenas that the reform truly happened. Cárdenas was ambitious and hoped to make the revolution work through the implementation of the main ideas of the Constitution of 1917. Among these were agrarian reform, subsoil rights, labor reform, state power over the church, and socialist education. His reforms were radical, but his delivery made them acceptable. Cárdenas traveled to remote rural villages to share with the peasants and *campesinos* his ideas about the land and who should control it. Between 1928 and 1932, Cárdenas allocated 141,663 hectares among 181 villages in Michoacán, a trend that spread throughout Mexico over the next decade. (Gonzales 2002).

In 1935, Hacienda Kantó and other area haciendas were dismantled in the wake of the major land reform that was finally coming to Yucatán. This was the last state in the Mexican Republic to realize tangible changes in the hacienda system. Kantó, located in the present-day municipality of Temozón, was populated by approximately 50 Maya *peones* (peons), a small number in comparison to haciendas in the henequen-growing zone in the northwest part of the state that had as many as 1,500–2,000 workers and their families living within their boundaries (Katz 2014; Wells and Joseph 1996; Littlefield 1978). Kantó was owned by C. Francisco Cantón, governor of Yucatán from 1898 to 1902, and was engaged in a mix of agriculture and livestock, growing corn and beans and raising grazing cattle (Cabrera Valenzuela 2013; Wells and Joseph 1996). By 1936 a group of 28 *campesinos* had gathered to petition for their *ejidal* land grant (Cabrera Valenzuela 2013). Here, don Wiliam retells the early founding story of X'Kumil:

> Well, my father and my mother lived in X'Kumil, they lived there in X'Kumil, and that is where we grew up. We were not many, about 10 thatch houses. In this time, the time of my parents, they solicited the land. There was a president named Lazaro Cárdenas who helped the people, the campesinos who lived in the haciendas. He gave them the land and called it an *ejido*. For example, X'Kumil received a piece of land that is 767 hectares for the campesinos who wanted to live there and work the land. And so that is where we started. ~Don Wiliam [Transcriptions 2009-0612 (51:08)]

By 1942, X'Kumil's *ejidal* land grant was complete.

Article 27 of the Mexican Constitution outlines three forms of land tenure: small private property, *ejidos*, and agrarian communities. Luin Goldring (1996) provides a useful conceptual framework for understanding property rights in Mexico. He suggests that we conceive of property rights as a package, based on his recognition of the fact that wealth and power differences between *ejidos* and even within the same *ejido* will be determinants of who has access to the various elements of a package of property rights (Goldring 1996, 272). Goldring (1996,

274) further distinguishes between the official package based on documentation, policies, and programs and the actual package that involves the practice of property rights.

Under this *ejidal* law, land had to be worked by the *ejidatario* and could not be rented, sold, or left unused. The idea was that land would form a basis of subsistence for peasant families and would not become an economic commodity. Following this thinking, the law prohibited *ejidatarios* from possessing more than one piece of land and they were granted "use rights," not ownership of the land. Because of this, they were unable to sell their plots. Under the law, the *ejidal* assembly, which consists of all *ejidatarios* in a given *ejido*, could reassign the use rights for a particular plot if they felt the laws were not being followed. In addition to the individual plots of an *ejido* there are also common use areas, which are generally made up of pasture and woods and account for 77 percent of all *ejidal* holdings in Mexico (Nuijten 2003a). *Ejidal* use rights provide both social and economic benefits. At a basic level, *ejidal* land provides basic food security as well as access to participation in multiple government-sponsored programs, such as the Programa de Apoyos Directos al Campo (Program for Direct Assistance in Agriculture, PROCAMPO). PROCAMPO was instituted in 1994 as part of a government-sponsored effort to liberalize rural Mexico (Klepeis and Vance 2003). The many factors surrounding the social and economic benefits of maintaining use rights to *ejidal* land give *ejidatarios* additional political connections that often lead to domination of the community's political life.

After approximately twenty-five years of living in X'Kumil, some residents and local officials decided it was time for a change. The village was just outside the border of their *ejidal* lands, within the *ejido* of Temozón (figure 4.1).

This caused periodic conflicts with *ejidatarios* from Temozón. The location near the northern border of the *ejidal* land also made travel from the village to the milpas arduous:

> X'Kumil is a neighbor of Temozón, but there is no archaeological zone and there is no way to make a life there. Because of this, we couldn't do much there. When we were there we didn't even have an *ejidal* commissioner because no one knew anything . . . we knew only how to sign our names. I read no more than my studies to the second grade, no more than this. I read a story of Chichén Itzá, Mayapán, and Cobá . . . but we had no zone there. After I read this book I wanted to work with the people, but what we had there was no good for anything. All we had there was a cave. When the rain fell in this time the trash and everything would be there and the water would be dirty. We did not want to live there anymore and so we brought everyone here. ~Don Ruperto [Transcriptions 2009-0712 (31:14)]

In 1969, local authorities began exploring the *ejido* and looking for a new place to settle. In the location of their first settlement, there was no *cenote*, or

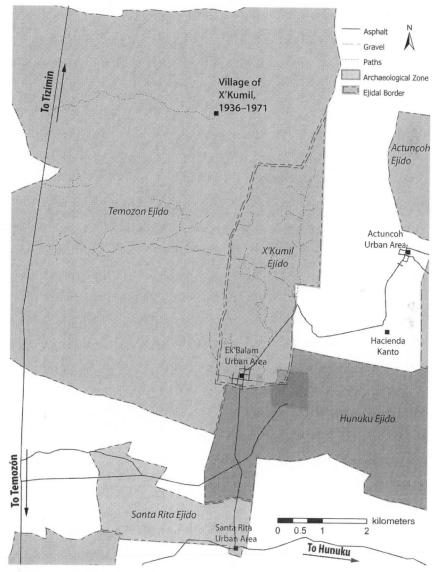

FIGURE 4.1. *Location of village of X'Kumil*

limestone sinkhole, from which they could access water. Their water came from a cave and was rarely clean. In addition, there were no good plots nearby to make their milpas, the land cultivated to grow corn, and so they had to travel a long way each day to work in their fields. In the process of soliciting the land for the *ejido* in the 1940s, the original *ejidatarios* did not know to ask for additional land for the village site (Cabrera Valenzuela 2013). Because of this, the village of

X'Kumil was located on land in the *ejido* of Temozón. Don Wiliam explained why this was a problem and why it was important for the population to move to a new location:

> I finished my primary school, and in this time I was young and I began analyzing the forest and the situation we had, and when I looked at the *ejidal* documents I saw that we did not have a place in the *ejido* set aside for the pueblo. And so I got up and started talking to people when I was only 17 years old. And I told them, "Why did you not ask for an endowment, a piece of land set aside for the pueblo of X'Kumil?" And they told me "well, we failed there; we did not know that this was something we needed because we did not have the understanding." Some began to say that we should just live together with the people of Temozón, but this is not recommendable, because the people of Temozón should have their land and the people of X'Kumil should have their own. And so I asked my father and the other *ejidatarios* "Why don't we make plans to form a village in this *ejido*?" And others helped me and said, "Well, let's go make these plans." So we got ourselves up and went to Mérida to see the agency that attended to the *campesinos*, which at that time was the Office of Agrarian Reform, and we asked them if we could form a village so that the people could separate and work apart from those in Temozón. And they explained to us what to do, but that we would have to use land from inside our own *ejido*, they could not give up any more land. And so we designated this place where we are now, Ek'Balam. ~Don William [Transcriptions 2009-0612 (01:04:19)]

There are multiple reasons for the move from X'Kumil to Ek'Balam. The ongoing conflict with *ejidatarios* from Temozón was probably the most important, followed closely by the existence of a functioning well. It is interesting that residents now offer the existence of the archaeological zone as part of the rationale for relocating where they did. It is not possible to know whether residents would have given this as a factor prior to the initial mapping and excavation at the archaeological zone of Ek'Balam. While some hail Mexico's agrarian reform as a victory for the country's huge indigenous population, others see it as yet another way in which the state created, dominated, and then pacified Indians (Friedlander 2006). Orthon Baños Ramírez (1989) hypothesizes that because of the state's failure to modify certain structures in place during the colonial period, agrarian reform is little more than a new bureaucracy overlaid on an inequitable social system.

REVISING LAND REFORM

For at least 3,000 years, people have been farming the Yucatán Peninsula, introducing species from other regions, and constructing terraced and ditched gardens to protect the species they found useful (Faust, Anderson, and Frazier 2004).

Multiple forces have changed these interactions, including agrarian reform, tourism, and development initiatives. In the mid-twentieth century, farming in North America shifted from an important and useful human endeavor to a branch of the business world. In Mexico's *ejidal* sector, this shift came in the 1980s, as international pressures presented unending reports to the Mexican government confirming the low productivity of the *ejidal* system (Levy 1997; Dornbusch and Helmers 1991). Specifically, the World Bank determined that "the sector had become obsolete and characterized by productive inflexibility and increasing non-compliance with the sector's legal framework" (Soloaga and Lara 2008, 248). To open the Mexican economy, world economic agencies encouraged Mexico to completely restructure the *ejidal* system, effectively ending decades of agrarian reform (Almazan 1997; Nuijten 2003b; Loewe and Taylor 2008).

The Agrarian Law of 1992 replaced the Federal Agrarian Reform Law of 1971 as part of the major reforms required for Mexico's participation in the North American Free Trade Agreement (NAFTA). This affected multiple issues with regard to land tenure in Mexico's agrarian sector. The most important of these changes are the following: no additional lands would be expropriated to create new *ejidos* or augment existing *ejidal* holdings; *ejidatarios* have permission to rent, sell, buy, or lease land in an attempt to modernize the system of land tenure; *ejidatarios* can work with private enterprises and individual investors; and *ejidatarios* will receive individual land titles. The Programa de Certificacion de Derechos ejidales y Titulacion de Solares Urbanos (Program for Certification of *Ejidal* Rights and Titling of Urban Plots, PROCEDE) began approaching *ejidos* in 1994 to encourage them to go through the certification process (Baños Ramírez 1998; Zepeda Lecuona 2003). Once all of the land in an *ejido* has been titled, the assembly can vote to move into *pleno domino*, or private ownership, and can only maintain its *ejidal* status if at least 20 percent of *ejidal* members want to remain as such. PROCEDE was a vehicle for the mapping and measurement of boundaries and registration of plots, both of which are widely regarded as neo-liberal policies that will improve land markets and the legal security of those lands (Nuijten 2003a; Bonilla Jimenez, Villa Aguijosa, and Orozco Plascencia 2010).

The municipality of Temozón is home to approximately 15,000 people. The municipal seat is the town of Temozón, with a population of 5,121. The remaining 10,000 people live in communities spread throughout the municipality (INEGI 2010). The municipality covers 1087.06 km2, of which 35 percent is in *ejidal* holdings. These 13 *ejidos* range in size from 22 to 365 *ejidatarios* and are located throughout the municipality (figure 4.2). Each one varies in the amount of land converted from communal land into individual parcels during PROCEDE (INEGI 2003). The amount of parceled—or privatized—land in the *ejidos* of Temozón averages 60.57 percent. This is a variation from the much lower statewide average of 31.47 percent (Registro Agrario Nacional 2015).

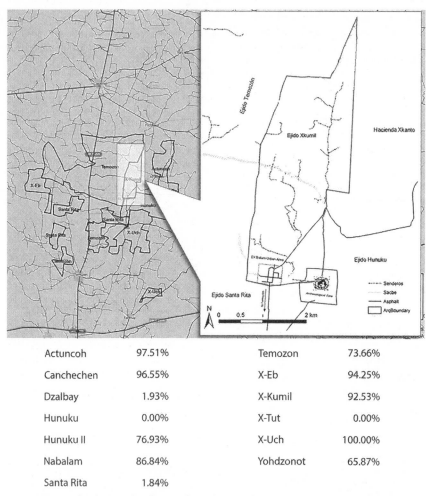

Actuncoh	97.51%	Temozon	73.66%
Canchechen	96.55%	X-Eb	94.25%
Dzalbay	1.93%	X-Kumil	92.53%
Hunuku	0.00%	X-Tut	0.00%
Hunuku II	76.93%	X-Uch	100.00%
Nabalam	86.84%	Yohdzonot	65.87%
Santa Rita	1.84%		

FIGURE 4.2. *Ejido of X'Kumil and rates of parcelization throughout the municipality of Temozón*

X'Kumil was one of first *ejidos* in Yucatán to go through PROCEDE's titling process (Registro Agrario Nacional 2015). To complete the process there must be a majority vote from the *ejidal* assembly. During the initial meetings in 1994, it became clear that this process would not be simple. Thirteen of the 26 *ejidatarios* wanted to parcel the *ejido* and the other 13 did not. The debate went back and forth over a period of a few weeks until the *ejidatarios* reached an agreement: they would divide the *ejido* into two pieces. The group that did not want to parcel consisted mostly of older *ejidatarios* who were accustomed to making milpa in larger areas of 100 to 150 mecates. After PROCEDE, each *ejidatario* would only have 24 hectares. Many of the younger *ejidatarios* saw great benefit in parceling, for various reasons. For some whose families relied very little on their *ejidal* tenure and were mostly engaged in migration or other economic strategies, PROCEDE meant they could sell their parcels. Although at this time the archaeological site had barely begun to attract visitors, some foresaw that there would soon be a demand for land near the site. Individuals who spent much of their time working near the coast had met workers from other towns throughout the region. Those who were from *ejidos* near the coast had already seen the inflated prices people were able to get for their land. These stories trickled back to Ek'Balam, where residents listened with great interest.

The *ejidal* assembly presented the decision to divide the *ejido* to PROCEDE; of the 21 *ejidatarios* present, 16 voted to parcel the *ejido* and 5 voted against it (Cabrera Valenzuela 2013). Discussion ensued, and there was a tenuous decision that they would title the new *ejido* in the names of the 16 men who were in favor of the process. When the decision was reached and the *ejidal* assembly adjourned, the 16 pro-PROCEDE *ejidatarios* went to Temozón to purchase supplies. After their return, they set off to mark a border. The 5 *ejidatarios* against the division accompanied them. Somewhere during the process, the group realized that regardless of how evenly the *ejido* was divided, there was no equitable way to ensure that both halves were even in all manners. The only way to accomplish this would have been to divide the village. Among the *ejidatarios* opposed to the division were 4 of the village founders who had made the move from X'Kumil to Ek'Balam. The others were children of these men and of the 2 deceased village founders. They remembered vividly the discord the village faced before leaving X'Kumil. According to don Fede:

> So they sat us down, those old men, and they said "enough of this, we're stopping right here!" Pues, we stopped there right in the middle of the *ejido*, almost half way through with cutting the new border. Don Delfino spoke first. He asked the youngest of us, Daniel and Lucio, if they knew why we moved from X'Kumil to Ek'Balam. These two were born in Ek'Balam. It was their home, and they didn't remember X'Kumil at all. They didn't remember the time when we had no school and no electricity. Between [*sic*] Don Delfino, Don Ruperto, and Don Gute they told us the history again. Whew, we heard that story a lot! But at the end they said that the younger had learned more and were more educated. They said that if we all thought that this was the right thing to do, then they were in agreement with their sons. They could not be stubborn enough to break up the town, because they knew that they would have to be the ones to leave, and that their wives and children would not want to. ~Don Federico [Transcriptions 2011–0102 (52:00)]

The next morning, the group members returned from their venture and spread the word that they would not divide the *ejido*. PROCEDE came ready to parcel and title half of X'Kumil, and the agent from the Office of Agrarian

Reform came ready to map the *ejido*. When they arrived, the assembly told them they would parcel the entire *ejido*.

With the arrival of tourism, land in Ek'Balam has taken on a new value. What was once a necessary resource for agriculture and space to build homes is now a commodity gaining the attention of outsiders, both foreigners and people from elsewhere in Mexico. This process accelerated between 2004 and 2012, demonstrated by a dramatic increase in outside ownership within the *ejido*. In 2004, individuals from outside the community owned two lots, for profiting from the increasing amount of tourists in the region. In 2012, no fewer than nine lots in the *ejido* were owned by individuals from outside the community (figure 4.3).

The question is, how are these changes in land use and ownership affecting members of the community as they attempt to continue farming on milpa lands and enjoy adequate land in the village for their homes? In 2004, many of the community members I spoke with had strong opinions about others selling their land; however, they realize that because the land is parceled, it is the right of each individual to do so:

> Now, in the time that we are in, it is a little complicated. You know why? In my role as *ejidal* commissioner, I cannot tell people that they cannot sell their land to tourists or foreigners. But with time, they will see that the land is going. There will not be a place for their children to live in the pueblo.

> For example, this is my son and his newborn son. In 20 years, more or less, this child will not have land. Because many people are coming, the tourists are coming here. They want to have a life here in Ek'Balam. There are people selling their own property. This, well, later where are their children going to live? Where are they going to make their milpas or the *palapas* of their sons or daughters? Why does this happen? For money. But there are people selling their parcels. The *ejidal* parcel is an inheritance. If I decided to sell my parcel, what would I give to my children and grandchildren? You see, we are multiplying. We are growing but the land is not. For this reason, I am careful with the parcel that I have, for the inheritance of my children and grandchildren.

> Sometimes a person comes looking for a piece of land. I, as *ejidal* commissioner, have to call an assembly of the *ejidatarios*. Then we have to decide if we can donate the land to this person who is soliciting us. But sometimes the person will already have a parcel and they will have sold it. The people say that 10 meters from the main road, they can ask 20,000 pesos for this. The person who comes here from [a]far, well this is cheap for them!

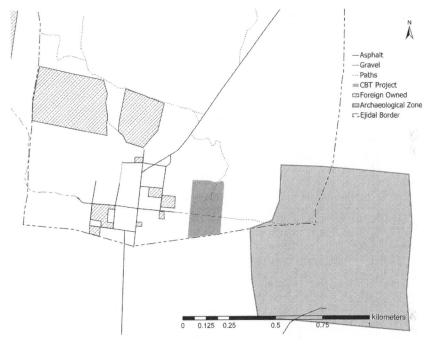

FIGURE 4.3. *Foreign-owned lots in ejido of X'Kumil, 2012*

For example, the story of Joan. She wanted to buy a big piece of land. The land that she has is about 2,000 square meters. She bought her land for 20,000 pesos. For her, about 2,000 dollars, right? And so there is an example of why this is happening. But, God willing, the people will think first. That they will hold on to their lands because more people are going to come here from other countries. If they keep coming and buying, well, good for the person selling, but it does not have a benefit for the pueblo. Only personal benefit. They are selling their children's futures. ~Don Rafael [Transcriptions 2004-0802]

This passage is representative of the sentiment found in most of the interviews I conducted. Because more people are coming to the region, outsiders are becoming aware of the business opportunities available. Don Rafael's concern that his sons may not have land to work when they come of age is a stress felt throughout the community. Based on this passage, the going price for land in 2004 was approximately US$4,047 per acre. By 2007, the price had changed significantly, according to the individuals interviewed. By 2012, the price per acre had skyrocketed. In that year a 1-acre lot in Ek'Balam listed for $140,000 Mexican pesos, or approximately US$14,000.

Since the beginning of the tourism boom on the Caribbean coast of the Yucatán Peninsula, many residents of rural areas have been migrating to this region to look for work. While the village of Ek'Balam did not have large numbers of young men leaving for employment, the numbers were steadily increasing. According to one of the men in the village:

> Many . . . many people are going to look for more for their lives. The truth is that in this time the life that we are living is a little different than before. Before there were only *campesinos*, all of the people went to the campo to work. In this time now it is not like this. Many want to go work in a city as a driver or in construction. This is what the men are looking for, but what they find there is dependence on the money, on drugs, whatever. Before it was not like this . . . we all planted, worked, burned our milpas. Now no. Also there are people dying on the road to Cancún. It is very dangerous. Sometimes when they are returning on Saturdays and drinking a little they crash. Almost no one wants to work in the campo now. The old system is leaving. Some feel that it is because there is not enough land to work. Now there are no forests like before. They too have gone because now we are many. Watch on Mondays all of the men who go to look for their lives. Most are married and want to make money for their wives. So, they go to Cancún. But Cancún is changing too, there used to be mountains of work there but now not as much. People from all over Mexico have gone there to work, not just Yucatecos.
> ~Don Rafael [Transcriptions 2010-12-22]

In 2004, many individuals expressed concern over the number of young men who were leaving the village for work. There were concerns with regard to the changes the village was experiencing but also concerns for the safety of the migrants. This was repeated multiple times in the interviews: "There are people who go. There is not money here. But it's dangerous. Sometimes they return and sometimes they don't. If they crash they will never arrive in their pueblo again" ~Don Ruperto [Transcriptions 2009-0802].

Figure 4.4 shows how rates of migration have changed. Prior to 2003, 40 percent of the collaborator sample reported that work outside of Ek'Balam was a major source of income for their household. In 2004, 20 percent of the individuals in the collaborator sample reported that they or the head of their household had migrated to Cancún for employment in the prior year. In 2007, this number was reduced by almost half. The leaders of the CBT project state that this is a result of the employment provided by the project.

It is true that many men stopped traveling to the coast during the construction of the Cabañas. Still, the number of people migrating for work was too large for some members of the community, who felt that leaving for work in Cancún translated to the young men not valuing the way of life in the village:

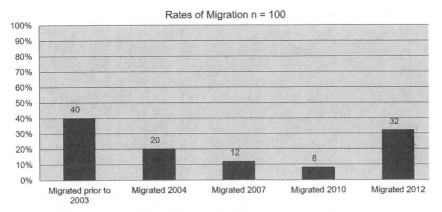

FIGURE 4.4. *Rates of migration, prior to 2003 through 2012*

Many of the things that have changed are because the people have gone to other places, Cancún, Mérida, distant places where there are other examples for them to copy and when they come back here, they have already seen the other forms. What they see in other places is what they practice, and so really, they feel superior, or different, things that they might not say. But us as the people here should not forget our customs and traditions. In one month, that someone goes to Cancún they return like this. They have begun to forget. The people who are going now are the ones who were unhappy and do not want to return to their land, they do not want to continue practicing that which we have here. ~Don Ruperto [Transcriptions 2009-0802]

When I explored further and asked questions about who had previously migrated but had once again settled in the village full-time, I found that prior to 2003 twice as many people worked outside the village as the number in 2004. I inquired further about these numbers and found that 2004 was the year the Cabañas was completed and opened for business and the year the Hotel Eden started attracting guests. In 2007, the number of individuals relying on migration as a primary earning strategy had dropped almost by half again, down to 12 percent of the collaborator sample. These figures were encouraging to some of the older individuals in the community, especially those who are working closely with the Cabañas project:

Actually, there are not so many from here that go to the coast these days. Here in Ek'Balam, right now we have a little work, like with the many projects we are doing and with Joan. Because of this, we do not have too many going to Cancún. The people who are going now are the ones who were unhappy and do not want to return to their land, they do not want to continue practicing that which we have here. What they like is a more active life where they can do many different things. We only have right now about two vehicles that go to Cancún, it is minimal. And this is encouraging for those of us who work with our project, because if we can create something that will allow our sons to stay here and not have to go look for their lives, well, this would be very good. ~Don Felipe [Transcriptions 2007-0718 (48:56)]

Based on the levels of migration reported in 2004 and 2007, the CBT project and other touristic endeavors in the village are having the desired effect of creating employment in there and alleviating the need for individuals to leave to earn enough money. In addition to work at the Cabañas, Hotel Eden, Dolcemente, Kaxil Kan, or Casa del Alux, construction work for the various outsiders who have purchased land and need it to be cleared and built on is an increasingly common form of employment also linked to the presence of tourism in the village. In 2010, the number of those leaving dropped even lower, to 8 percent. Some still attribute this to the success of tourism in Ek'Balam, though others say it happened because of the economic crisis that started with the H1N1 Influenza scare in 2009. These changing household earning strategies depend on cultural capital in ways I address in chapter 5. The ability to diversify these strategies is what has always maintained households in Ek'Balam.

Development in a Community in Crisis

The quest for "community" has been called an obsession by some and a failure by others. What can be agreed on is the fact that it has been an important, if troublesome, force driving development, scholarship, theory, and practice. Gerald W. Creed (2006, 23) traces the progression of "community" as a concept, a romantic notion, and, finally, as "modern pastoral." Victor W. Turner introduces a discussion of structure, *communitas*, and *societas*. *Communitas* is defined as a model of human relations that emerges in a liminal phase and is characterized by a lack of structure and communion of individuals in this liminal state who are connected by their collective role as submissive to the dominant authority (Turner 1995, 127). What is interesting here is the further discussion of *communitas* and its distinction from "community." With the current interest in defining "community"—whether to espouse its virtue or critique its shortcomings as a unit of analysis—Turner's discussion remains relevant more than forty years later. Turner makes a broad definition of possible units of social structure as "relationships between statuses, roles, and offices" (Turner 1995, 130).

DOI: 10.5876/9781607327721.c005

The community-based approach to development takes for granted the fact that there is a community in which to base the project or initiative. The consideration of community is nothing new in Mesoamerica. Early in the history of Mesoamerican ethnography, the community emerged as the central form of social organization into which all "peasant-Indians" could be classified and all behavior understood. As John Monaghan (1999) commented, the triad of the "Indian peasant community" is as ubiquitous in ethnographies from the region as are discussions of corn, beans, and squash. The systematic ethnographic study of community in Mesoamerica has contributed significantly to the conceptual study of communities in other culture areas. Mesoamerica presents an interesting case for many reasons. Hugo G. Nutini (1996, 81) commented that in Mesoamerica the community had "long ceased to be part of the tribe but was not yet part of the nation."

Chapter 4 discussed some of the factors contributing to the economic rationale found in Mesoamerica's small, rural, agrarian villages. Many generalizations and comparisons are made across the various regions and nation-states. For instance, Sheldon Annis's (1987) discussion of milpa logic in the Guatemalan highlands echoes Alan R. Sandstrom's (1991) work in Amatlan, and Frank Cancian's (1992) argument that change is leading to the decline of community is similar to Guillermo de la Peña's (1982) work. At the same time, it is also important to recognize the differences between regions in Mesoamerica. Many of these differences relate directly to the political borders that separate the nations. Where the different regions of the Maya World are similar is in the role of "community," however defined, in the processes of tourism development, commodification of indigeneity, and anthropological research.

In the case of tourism development in Ek'Balam, the accepted models for community development seem to be failing. This chapter presents reasons for this and other failings of the "little community" ideal of development and builds on the discussion of community as an object of study by explaining its current positioning as an object of development. The economic processes surrounding the development of the Yucatán Peninsula as an international tourism destination were part of a larger shift toward neo-liberalism seen throughout Latin America and even the world (Clancy 2001a; Warren and Jackson 2003; Van den Berghe 1994). Here, a brief history of development and anthropology's engagement with it provides a context for understanding how the community-based model came into fashion and use. We will come to see that a community is rarely what it seems from the outside. The Ay Mena family will again help us understand the ways Ek'Balam both resembles and differs from the community imagined by the agencies funding the community-based tourism (CBT) project.

The air outside this afternoon is hot, dry, and relentless. It has not rained yet, and people are beginning to worry that the rains will not come in time to water the tiny corn plants before they wither. Doña Goma just returned from the Diconsa store with 10 kilos of maize. The Tiendas Comunitarias Diconsa (Diconsa Community Stores) program aims to improve nutritional capacity in Mexico's rural communities of between 200 and 2,500 residents. This program came to Ek'Balam in 2008 and has been very well received. There was not much of a harvest last year because of the lack of rainfall, so the Ay Mena family must purchase a large portion of their corn this year. Fortunately, Diconsa just announced that it would not raise the price of white corn this year as had been feared. I ask Doña Goma how they are able to afford the maize, and she replies, "We can't. We are in crisis because of the sickness that they are talking about." It has been two months since the H1N1 Influenza (Swine Flu) outbreak, and everyone is feeling the effects. Goma has not sold one hammock in two months, and there have been very few village tours. They are cutting corners everywhere they can. She returned to Hotel Eden to ask Joan if she needs help with the laundry or cleaning, but Joan is barely able to stay open this summer and does not have the resources to take on any additional employees. Last week, she had to cut her staff to a bare minimum.

The house and yard are noticeably quiet these days. Eugenio is still in Cancún working, although there is not work for him every day and some weeks he does not work at all. This means he comes home less frequently and brings less money for the family when he does. Salvador left last week for the coast to find work with his brother. Eugenio said his boss was looking for additional people for a different job, so Salvador will be able to make a little money. He graduated from secondary school in Temozón earlier in the summer and planned to go on to high school. He took the exams and registered to begin in September. After seeing what the H1N1 epidemic was doing to the village, Salvador decided that school was too expensive and told his parents he would not go. While no residents have been infected with this strain of flu, the outbreak is deterring most tourists from traveling in Mexico. At the same time, those who are here are spending less because of the economic crisis. This is affecting even households that are still farming because last winter there was an infestation of worms in the milpas, decreasing the harvest to nearly nothing. So at only age seventeen, Salvador joined Eugenio in Cancún.

Don Lucas rides up on his bike to the Almendra tree where Goma and I are enjoying the shade. She is weaving a hammock with brown and olive-green thread. Don Lucas thinks these colors are awful and tells her as much, but most women in the village maintain that having a military green hammock is the best way to make a sale. They know that gringos wear this color and that these are the most frequently purchased hammocks.

Don Lucas joins us and shares his news. He just returned from Temozón, where he went to work for the day fixing a roof. On the way home he stopped at doña Flora's house to check on Rosa, their eldest daughter. Last month she eloped with a man from the village. This devastated both families and created a high degree of tension in the village. Modesto, Rosa's husband, is the son of don Ignacio Cruz and doña Filomena. Ignacio Cruz was one of the associates of the CBT project but dropped out a few months ago. While don Lucas is not one of the project's leaders, interactions between Ignacio Cruz and the remaining associates are tense. The Dzib Tuz family is large, and Modesto's eldest sister is married to don Lucas's younger brother. They have separated themselves from Lucas's family to such an extent that when his mother fell ill last winter, they refused to contribute money to her medical bills. When a young couple elopes, it creates a dramatic situation, suddenly joining two families who have had no time to consider the idea of the union. Rosa and Modesto have been sent to live with doña Filomena for the time being while their parents cool off.

With the three eldest children gone, only Federico, Nacho, and Vanessa remain. Federico is sixteen and is working with one of the groups in the volunteer summer camp. The Conservation Corps of Yucatán (CCY) is holding another summer camp program. Thirty-five college students from all across Mexico, South America, and Spain are in the village for this three-week program. They are divided into teams and take turns working on the four community development projects initiated for the camp: adobe stoves, nature trails, a community museum, and an art project for the children. Each team has children of the CBT project's associates on it as part of the program's participatory nature. Federico and his friends love it. The program was not initially designed to attract only the young men in the village, but because it is inappropriate for young women to run around town with strangers, none of the associates let his daughters join the teams. Since the camp started two weeks ago, Federico only comes home to eat and bathe. Two nights ago he spent the whole night with the volunteers at the commissary building in the center of town. All of them are camping out there, and their local teammates are spending increasing amounts of time with them. His parents were upset, but they see how much he is enjoying himself and so let it be. Whenever someone asks where Federico is, don Lucas replies that he is at the party. "It is always a party in Ek'Balam now," he comments.

Nacho, in contrast, is uninterested in anything that has to do with the Cabañas, the volunteers, or tourists in general. This is the first time the two boys have not been spending most of their days together. Nacho brushes this off, though, and talks about how happy he is working in the milpa. The crisis forces Lucas to take any chamba (odd job) that comes up, so Nacho has been responsible for much of the agricultural work this season. He is as worried as his father is about the lack of rain.

It feels as though the heat is making each day longer and more difficult than usual. Many households are in the midst of conflicts, which is all the more apparent because don Lucas is currently serving as the police deputy. In the last two weeks, someone coming to him about a conflict or altercation has awakened the household in the night many times. The crisis caused by the *"enfermedad que dicen"* (the sickness they are talking about) extends beyond financial woes and into village social life. There are numerous allegations of *brujería* (witchcraft) made against the Dzib kin group, and this has everyone on edge. One member of the Tuz kin group died unexpectedly in May, and another young man is gravely ill. Some residents whisper that Hilario Dzib Tuz is a Way Miis and blame him for these afflictions. The story of the *way* is common throughout Yucatán. In short, the *way* is a human who can take the shape of various animals to conduct nefarious activities in the night. In the case of don Hilario, he is accused of taking on the form of a *miis* (cat) to move unseen through the night and enter houses of the Tuz kin group. Others believe the entire kin group is at fault and swap stories about sighting his grandmother with playing cards or other items associated with black magic and of the unexplained vigor of her flowers in this time of drought. *Chisme caliente* (hot gossip) rises up from all corners of the village and blows around on the hot, dry breeze.

The contrast between the animated activities of the volunteer camp and the strained interactions among many residents is striking. I comment on this, and don Lucas tells me it is *la canícula*. This is high summer when the ground is nearly bone dry. These are the dog days. *La canícula* makes everyone a bit harried as they hope for rain. The prospects are not good, according to him, because for the fifth consecutive summer the village will not hold a Ch'a Chaak ceremony to call down the rains.

The heat is keeping everyone from being industrious, and we are content to keep our activities confined to the shade of the Almendra tree. Nacho unties a bundle from the back of his bicycle and lays it out on the ground. He returned just before lunch from spending all morning in the milpa collecting the vines he is now untangling. He and don Lucas set about cutting them in various lengths, and doña Goma instructs me to get my camera and notebook. She is sure I will want to take pictures and write about this. Don Lucas is teaching Nacho how to make a *xux*, a large cylindrical basket used for harvesting maize. It is carried on a person's back by a tumpline across the forehead. Nacho is animated and clearly waited some time for his father to teach him this craft. Not all men still make their own baskets, and it is a point of pride for don Lucas to teach his son to do so. Doña Goma wonders aloud if tourists would buy smaller versions of these baskets. Nacho responds gruffly, "What tourists? There aren't any more gringos here these days!"

One of the most common recurring themes in the ethnographic literature from Mesoamerica is change. Some have argued that the peasant is resistant to change, while others have presented him as agreeable to it. For Frank Cancian, change has been the preeminent theme running through the monographs he has written about the Tzotzil community of Zinacantan in the Chiapas highlands (Cancian 1965, 1972, 1992). There are numerous possibilities for why change has been such an important theme for him, one of which could be his early dependence on Eric R. Wolf's (1957) model for the closed corporate community. It is difficult for many communities to fit into this otherwise useful model. Cancian's (1965) early designation of Zinacantan as a closed corporate community has framed his work since then and led him to see the economic shifts and "opening" of the community over time as not symptomatic of the numerous changes happening at the global level but as specific signposts of a declining community (Vogt 1969).

The fact that Cancian focused on community as an object of study is not surprising. As he states, "In 1960 anthropologists studied communities with as much regularity as Zinacantecos wore their costumes" (Cancian 1992, 1). His fieldwork there continued through the 1970s, when the focus shifted from community to world systems, and ideas about the peasantry became complicated by capitalist relations of production and the role of peasants in political economy. These factors illuminate his reasoning for examining change; not only was life in the village altered, but his theoretical inclinations were in the process of major change. The common perception of indigenous groups as slow to change, backward, and undeveloped or underdeveloped has led to a general approach by the state that assumes little change on the part of indigenous communities. Sol Tax (1957, 158), in contrast, argues that "developing communities need the freedom of the marketplace and a good display of merchandise from which to choose, and no salesman."

The community emerged in Mesoamerican ethnographic studies as the most useful and common unit of analysis early in the proliferation of peasant village studies. Among the first to begin the proliferation of those studies were Eric Wolf (1955, 1957), Robert Redfield (1941; Redfield and Villa Rojas 1934), Oscar Lewis (1947, 1960), and Frank Cancian (1965, 1972). In addition to attempting to classify individuals as peasant, *campesino*, and Maya, various ethnographers attempted to create the community and its particularities as bounded entities for study. For example, Tax (1937) used linguistic classifications and administrative designation of the municipality to refer to groups and imply ethnic difference. He saw the *municipio* (municipality) as both an ethnic and a geographic unit. The use of the existing political and geographic designation created for Tax (1937) a tangible unit by which he could better deal with the study of communities.

In contrast to this early work by Tax, Wolf (1955) emphasized the need for historicizing ethnographic research and acknowledging that the community cannot be a static category because it is influenced by political and economic interactions both externally and within a particular community. Similarly, George M. Foster (1943) discussed the ways the Popoluca were categorized and found that while they were originally thought to be one group based on geographic and linguistic affiliations, it was in fact discovered that they were multiple groups, or what he called a "conquest culture." With this, Foster effectively brought identity into the process of defining units of analysis for study in Mesoamerica.

Cancian also used the community as a unit in his early research; however, in later publications he stated that by the mid-1970s, ideals about the peasantry had been transformed by capitalist relations of production, state relations, and the role of the so-called peasant in the national and international political economy (Cancian 1992). With this and similar assertions by other ethnographers, it became clear that the community was not an adequate unit for study in the Maya World. Indeed, a number of scholars have noted the difficulty of relating local cultures to larger national and even international systems within anthropology (M. Fischer and Marcus 1986; Knorr-Cetina and Harré 1981). In many cases, external influences were considered secondary to the local situation, yet at the same time the macro–world systems perspective was guilty of presuming that all change moved from the core to the periphery and that there was no generation of change happening at the local level. Later, Edward F. Fischer (2001, 6) argued for a middle ground between these two extremes by suggesting that Maya individuals be seen as "actively seeking their self-conceived best interests while working within larger systems not entirely of their own making."

To begin a discussion of wealth differences among peasant societies, one must first look at local determiners of wealth. This is one of the critical missed steps in many early community studies throughout Mesoamerica because if an emic definition of wealth is not established, then the community as a whole will be viewed as "poor." The concept of relative poverty is important to this process, as it aids in the identification of wealth. Oscar Lewis (1947) further argues that distribution is vital to understanding wealth and because so much wealth is gained through land, land tenure is of the utmost importance.

Orthon Baños Ramírez, following Arturo Warman (1988), defines *campesinos* as individuals who meet the following four criteria: (1) depend fundamentally on their work or labor; (2) maintain profound connections with the land, either directly or indirectly; (3) retain control over decisions made with regard to the production process; and (4) are integrated into community structures as individuals and as members of households (Baños Ramírez 1989). This definition does not, however, extend to *ejidatario* because that is a judicial term and status. This, according to Baños Ramírez (1995), has resulted in theoretically vacant investigations of *campesinos* living within the *ejidal* structure. Similarly, de la Peña (1982, 5–6) presents six characteristics of the peasantry, culled from scholarship throughout Mesoamerica: (1) transitional, (2) resilient to invasions from the outside world, (3) based on the household as production-consumption unit, (4) a result of the impact of wider society—especially capitalist society, (5) linked to the wider society through asymmetrical links, and (6) a mode of production that is articulated to other modes of production, especially capitalist ones, and often referred to as "petty-commodity." A main characteristic of this mode is "its inability to generate more capital than necessary simply to perpetuate itself" (de la Peña 1982, 7).

George Foster's (1965) concept of limited good is generally concerned with the nature of cognitive orientation and the way this is represented economically. Foster argues that because a peasant community is a closed system, the commonly accepted view is that all things exist in a finite quantity that cannot increase. What this means for members of a community is that increasing one's lot can only be done at the expense of another (Foster 1965, 296). Theoretically, this would drive peasants to either the extreme of maximum cooperation or individualism. Foster (1965, 301) states that the first choice is uncommon, as peasants always choose individualism. Following this logic, Foster calls for a change in the fundamental goals of development by working to change peasants' view of limited good rather than increasing achievement. The concept of limited good has been useful to Mesoamerican community studies, but it has also been roundly criticized. James R. Gregory and colleagues (1975) question whether limited good is a peasant worldview not of all goods and wealth but instead of their access to them. Further, John W. Bennett (1966) suggests a reversal of Foster's model by seeing limited good not as a typology but rather as a result of prolonged exploitation.

Wolf (1957, 1) defines the peasant as an "agricultural producer in effective control of land who carries on agriculture as a means of livelihood, not as a business for profit." Peasants are then organized into peasant communities with similar characteristics that "induce them to content themselves with the rewards of shared poverty" (Wolf 1957, 2). Residents of rural towns and villages (whether referred to as peasants, *campesinos*, or simply "rural poor") are shifting to a dependence on multiple earning strategies. This leads theorists such as Jeffrey D. Sachs (Sachs et al. 1995), Sarah Whatmore (1993), and others to concede that rurality cannot be confined to a descriptive term for agricultural producers. Rural residents throughout Mesoamerica were long thought to be engaging mostly in penny capitalism (Tax 1972); however, Cornelia Butler Flora (1990) "argues that global monetary and fiscal policies now assume more importance than trade in rural-urban relations" (quoted in Sachs 1996, 143). This is surely the case in Ek'Balam, where many have given up on corn and are "farming" tourists.

Like the idea of community, rurality is a difficult notion to wrangle. Duncan MacLean Earle (1984) defines rural as the cultural predilection of maintaining a relationship between a household and a specific natural habitat. Alicia Re Cruz (1996) further complicates the definition of a rural Maya community with her study of families who travel back and forth from Cancún to Chan Kom. Their life in the city as laborers in the tourism trade surely disconnects them from the rural community defined by so many ethnographers in Mesoamerica; however, their maintenance of social and cultural ties to Chan Kom creates a situation in which households must straddle two lifestyles and two milpas (Re Cruz 1996).

Chan Kom is a Maya village just 70 kilometers south of Ek'Balam. In 1950 the village of Chan Kom was similar to Ek'Balam in many ways. The population was about 251 in 1934 and 437 in 1948, and there were five of what Redfield (1950) referred to as "great patrilineal families," which were among the village founders and maintained prominence in the community. According to Redfield (1950), the introduction of commerce—and consequently of competition for trade—creates a different situation compared to when everyone is involved in agricultural pursuits. He continues: "The subgroups of these Yucatecan villages and the anciently and persistently competitive groups are the great patrilineal families. If these families more or less co-operate for the common good, the village prospers. If they engage in bitter struggles with one another, the village cannot go forward" (Redfield 1950, 62). Reexaminations of Redfield's "little community" model brought into question the assumptions that came along with relying on the community as a category in ethnographic inquiry. The fact that it left little room for understanding internal stratification and sociopolitical power structures made the little community useful for evaluation only at the surface level.

COMMUNITY-BASED TOURISM AND THE LEGACY OF COMMUNITY

The intersection of the concern for community and its application to the arena of development is apparent through the observation that as the commons become resources, whether natural, cultural, or material, they are moved out of the domain of community and toward the market. This further confuses the concept, according to Arturo Escobar (1995). The unqualified definition of community assumes a lack of stratification within the target group and is too often used to "denote a culturally and politically homogenous social system or one that, at least implicitly, is internally cohesive and more or less harmonious" (Mansuri and Rao 2004, 8). A widely known example of this assumption is Redfield's (1941) "little community."

From the new tradition of participatory development comes the concept of community-based tourism (CBT) development. This approach is an attempt to use grassroots development practices and the cultural knowledge of stakeholders to create a tourism project whose benefits are widely dispersed among the "hosts" and whose aspects of marketing and cultural performance are negotiated and determined to be acceptable by the community. Some of the first attempts at CBT were integrated conservation and development projects (ICDPs).

These projects were part of the Wildlands and Human Needs Program, which was initiated by the World Wildlife Fund (WWF) in 1985. According to Larson, Freudenberger, and Wyckoff-Baird (1998, quoted in Stonich 2005, 80), the goal of these projects was "to improve the quality of life of rural people through practical field projects that integrated the management of natural resources with grassroots economic development." While ICDPs now represent over half of the WWF's funding allocations, in the 1980s they were practically unheard of. The WWF now separates the ICDPs into first-generation projects of the 1980s and second-generation projects undertaken in the 1990s and later (Stonich 2005, 80). The first-generation projects became large and unmanageable, similar to the rural development projects of the 1970s, and are now recognized as not very integrated (Stonich 2005, 80). The ICDPs of the second generation emerging in the 1990s were modified to incorporate a view of local people as the stewards of resource management. These projects were commonly referred to as community-based conservation projects; they attempted to provide for more community involvement and strengthened relationships between conservation and development (Stonich 2005, 82). The improvements in project design notwithstanding, this generation of ICDPs was criticized for some of the same things mentioned in critiques of community-based tourism development. Namely, they attempt to standardize concepts such as community, participation, and representation (Stonich 2005, 82), thus generalizing the needs and desires of the intended beneficiaries of a project into a "one size fits all" model.

The design and implementation of community-based tourism development clearly demonstrate the problematic use of "community" as a target of development and the unquestioned association between *ejido* and community. In Ek'Balam as in other community-based development projects throughout the region, the project was designed to use the existing *ejidal* structure in the village as the framework for determining who would participate in the project as part of "the community." All *ejidatarios* and their families were eligible to become associates of the project. They would then be involved in its construction, management, and maintenance in exchange for a share of the profits. The problem, however, begins with the fact that not every household in the village has an *ejidatario* associated with it. In a few cases, a woman brings her husband to live there because of economic factors or the need to care for an aging family member. The husband cannot become an *ejidatario*. Another reason a household may be landless has to do with the shifting land tenure system. Because it is now possible for individuals to sell all or part of their land, available plots for those who previously could have solicited land in the *ejido* to make their homes or milpas are decreasing. The fact that the community-based tourism project begins by limiting participation to *ejidal* members automatically excludes some residents from participation and, in turn, from benefit.

Among some sections of the community, however, there is much excitement about the CBT project. The employment it provides is of great importance to those directly benefiting from it, and they talk about the pride they feel when tourists come to stay there. The three men in charge of the organization are eager to improve their business and expand the services they can offer visitors and to actively seek the advice and assistance of both the National Commission for the Development of Indigenous Villages (CDI) and the Conservation Corps of Yucatán (CCY). The self-stated objectives of the project are to (1) take advantage of the flora and fauna of the region through eco-tourism, (2) create tourist attractions from the caves and *cenotes* used for religious ceremonies, (3) generate additional economic income for the community of Ek'Balam to stop the need for its residents to emigrate, and (4) become accustomed to providing good accommodations to local, national, and foreign visitors (CDI 2003).

With the construction of U Najil Ek'Balam, the village of Ek'Balam became the location of the CDI's pilot community-based tourism development project. In the years since its completion, the Cabañas project has had both success and failure. Originally, it was envisioned as a project that would benefit all members of the community, whether *ejidatarios* or otherwise. This changed once the project got under way and it was determined that the existing *ejidal* structure would serve well for implementing the project, so that only *ejidatarios* would benefit directly:

> The first was a grant from CDI. It was a grant for all of the inhabitants of this locality, because all of us deserve the help, even if they are not an *ejidatario*. The second came from CONAFOR [Mexican Forestry Agency]. They have helped us greatly. There still has not been any education for us though. This is one of the things that we are working on. The truth is that here almost no one has studied. Most no more than their grade school. We need to learn English, but it is hard . . . we are *campesinos* and we work. ~Don Rafael [Transcription 2009-0624 (11:21)]

The commitment on the part of participants involves a twenty-four-hour shift as *velador*, or guard, every eighteen days and the occasional donation of materials for upkeep of the structures and grounds through the provision of *guano*, or palm fronds, from their parcels for the thatch roofs and wood. By 2007, at least five families that were working with the project decided they no longer wanted to be involved. For some families in Ek'Balam the promised benefits ceased to justify the costs in time and, indirectly, in money. For the individuals and families who continue to work directly with the Cabañas, the project remains an important source of income and even pride for them, and they are eager to see it succeed. The attitude these individuals hold toward those who are not positive about the project is increasingly aggressive, as is the attitude of the latter to the former. In the three years between 2004 and 2007, numerous changes occurred that indicate this broader shift in relations between the families who are and who are not participating in the village's community-based tourism project.

I have spoken with members of the families who are no longer participating about how and why they made this choice. Some individuals were not comfortable discussing their decision and the reasoning behind it, which is understandable given the social pressures surrounding the project. Justino is a twenty-five-year-old man who is the grandson of one of the village founders. His father and grandfather decided to stop working with the CBT project in 2005. For most of the project's existence, they had questioned how widely it would benefit the community, but after the director of the association showed up with a large new truck, the two men decided they could no longer lend their effort to the project. When asked why the family left the project, this was Justino's reply:

> I read in the newspaper that they [project leaders] were sent lots of money by the government to build their Cabañas, but the people have not seen any of this. Only some of the people are working there, it is not good for everyone. They choose who they give money to and who not to . . . There are rumors going around that [the] new truck was bought with the money that was for the Cabañas and the *ejidatarios*. Most of the people say it is so . . . Hopefully we will be able to talk enough to stop this at some point. They are the only ones benefiting . . . they are very corrupt. For me and my father and my grandfather, we are not in agreement about this. It will not grow into a tourist area with them running things. I know that when you are talking with them you hear pretty things coming from their mouths, they speak well. But it is because they don't know you. They think "well, she has come to help us; maybe she will make Ek'Balam known to others." This is what I do not like about the pueblo. It makes me feel bad that it is like this in our pueblo. But it will never have big tourism if they do not change. With the grants they were supposed to bring people, but there are none . . . how will they pay for the Cabañas they built if no one comes? It would have been better if they didn't do it at all. ~Justino [Transcription 2005-0723 (37:04)]

The criticism from some members of the community notwithstanding, the leaders of the CBT project are positive about the progress they have made, as well as the effects the project has had on the community. According to them, there are three types of benefits: social, economic, and environmental. They state that the project has generated twenty-three full-time jobs and sixteen part-time jobs that indirectly benefit seventy families living in the community and that with this work they are able to integrate all members of the *ejido* into the project. According to official statements about the project made at a meeting with funders, the economic benefits have provided a better quality of life for residents based on income from the sale of handicrafts and touristic services. On the environmental front, they claim that the project has made the community more conscience about their natural resources; as such, many have begun to reforest their parcels with plants that are useful as both commercial products and for the improvement of the *monte* (forest) surrounding the village.

Regardless of the successes of the community's tourism project, participation declined by 24 percent in the three-year period between 2004 and 2007. Figure 5.1 shows that overall rates of participation dropped consistently between 2004 and 2012, to only 32.5 percent of the collaborator sample involved with the CBT project in 2012. The reported benefits of this project for the community as a whole vary depending on the source of information. While the leaders of the Cabaña project state that 70 families are receiving economic benefit from the project, I found this number was an exaggeration in light of actual levels of participation and sources of income.

Reported sources of income also imply that many households have no direct financial benefit from tourism in the village. The average number of individuals living in one household unit is 6.63. Multiplying this number by the 70 families purported to be benefiting from the Cabañas project gives a product of 464 individuals—more than the entire population of the village. A number that is more realistic for stating economic benefit is 70 individuals, or about 11 households.

This follows closely the data from the sample group regarding responses about participation in the project and kin group membership. As we see in figure 5.2, some kin groups have high levels of ongoing participation in the CBT project (Ay and May), while others reported sharp drops in participation during the same period. Participation among members of the Chan kin group fell by about 80 percent, and participation among the Dzb kin group fell from 85 percent to zero between 2004 and 2012. The decline seen in the Lopez kin group was less drastic, at around 43 percent.

DOMINATION OF THE "LITTLE COMMUNITY"

The phenomenon of elite capture or domination as demonstrated here is particularly troublesome in the implementation and execution of community-based development initiatives. The operationalized definition of community-based projects centers on the control over the design, implementation, and management staying in the hands of "the Community." As mentioned earlier, the use of this term without qualification fails to account for the local structures—social, economic, and political—that are of great importance to the success of a project and the fruition of any rhetoric regarding shared benefit. Avoiding or overlooking this important aspect in the planning and implementation phases of a project inevitably leads to what Mansuri and Rao (2004) refer to as elite domination.

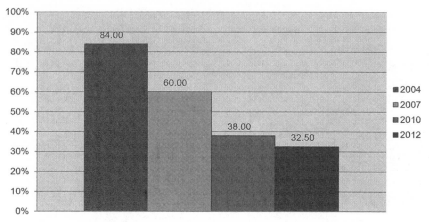

FIGURE 5.1. *Change in CBT participation within collaborator sample, 2004–2012*

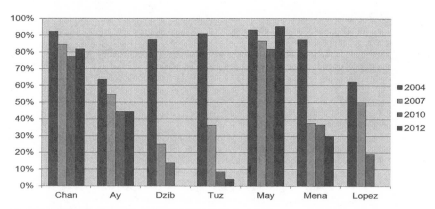

FIGURE 5.2. *Levels of participation in CBT project by kin group, 2004–2012*

An interesting point in keeping with these statements is that the reported levels of participation in tourism outside of the CBT project—through the sale of handicrafts, employment in a tourism business, or employment at the archaeological zone—do not mirror the levels of participation in the project (figure 5.3). In fact, those levels rose consistently over the 2004–12 period, with the category "Crafts" increasing by 32 percent among the collaborator sample.

Excursions to Temozón are common, especially among men looking for chamba (work doing odd jobs). There are many more opportunities for temporary employment there than in Ek'Balam or one of the other nearby villages. Among the jobs the men perform are constructing houses, clearing land, mending fences, working cattle, and generally doing anything else they can find. This is an important source of income during most of the year, particularly in the

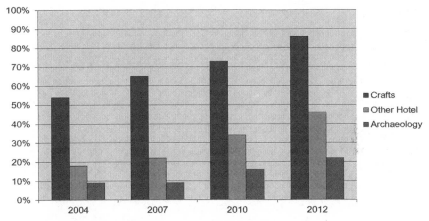

FIGURE 5.3. *Household income from tourism outside of CBT project, 2004–2012*

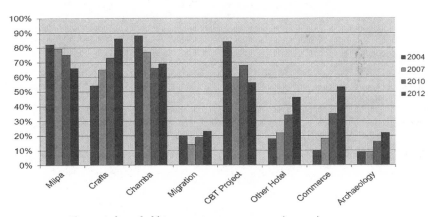

FIGURE 5.4. *Change in household income sources, 2004–2012 (n = 100)*

summer when most people's stores of corn have been exhausted and they must purchase bags of it.

Working the milpa is the most important activity for the majority of residents in Ek'Balam. Figure 5.4 shows the eight most important sources of income found in the community and the change over the period 2004 to 2012. The data for each category are based on the responses of individuals in the collaborator sample when asked if this was a significant source of income for their household. Diverse economic strategies are important to a household's success, and all households without exception are reliant on any number of these sources of income at a given time. To provide an illustration of this, in 2004, 82 percent of the collaborator sample listed "Milpa" as one of their sources of income. Of that 82 percent, most also listed additional sources of income.

The category "Crafts" is reported by anyone who produces and sells crafts for sale to tourists (e.g., hammocks, embroidered blouses). The category "Chamba" includes all odd jobs, as previously mentioned. These jobs are often outside the village, but this category differs from migration in that the workers come home each day after work. Rarely does chamba refer to steady work. "Migration" is the designation given to anyone who spends at least half of his time outside the village for the purpose of employment and maintains some sort of residence outside the village. The category "CBT Project" includes anyone who reported participation in the project. This includes the *ejidatarios* who are participating in the community's tourism project, as well as members of their families who have either indirect benefit from the fact that the head of their household works there or who have direct income from working there themselves. "Other Hotel" includes any individuals who reported having income from Hotel Eden, Dolcemente, Casa del Alux, or Kaxil Kan. These are the four tourism establishments in the village apart from the CBT project. This also includes members of the household that are part of the village tour offered to guests at Hotel Eden.

The category "Commerce" is used to represent individuals who have income from some form of commerce in which they are directly involved. This mainly includes individuals who sell goods from their homes. Examples of items sold are snacks, sodas, water, and produce. The selection of goods available in stores ranges from simple offerings of soda, gum, and snacks to the extensive offerings in one store that include items ranging from batteries and laundry detergent to toilet paper and rope and all manner of packaged snack foods. "Archaeology" refers to work at the archaeological zone that individuals are currently performing and excludes previous work during the initial excavation because the majority of men were involved in that activity. Positions currently held include guides and security duty, both during the day and at night, and since 2011, construction and maintenance of protective thatch coverings for the stuccoes.

To understand the relationship between the idealized project benefits and the actual rate of gain experienced by members of the community, I would like to revisit the study of Chan Kom by Robert Redfield (1950; Redfield and Villa Rojas 1934) and the reinterpretation of this study by Victor Goldkind (1965). In 1948, Redfield returned to Chan Kom to follow up on his previous study and report on the changes that had taken place over the seventeen-year period. Much of what he reported with regard to the levels of social stratification had remained unchanged during this period. Goldkind's reinterpretation of Redfield's study focuses on the claims made by Redfield and Villa Rojas (1934) and later Redfield (1950) that the village of Chan Kom is made up of a homogenous group of Maya and that while "differences in status do exist [they] lie simply between one person and another. There are no social classes" (Redfield and Villa Rojas 1934, 101). According to Goldkind's (1965, 883) reinterpretation of Redfield's data, "Some degree of

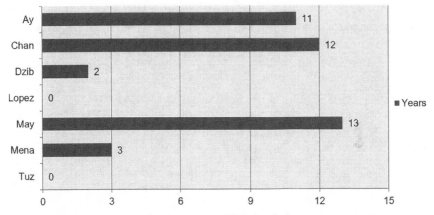

FIGURE 5.5. *Years as municipal commissioner of Ek'Balam by kin group, 1971–2012*

structural heterogeneity deriving from the social stratification system . . . should be postulated as a basic characteristic of this type of community."

The utility of this example can be understood by applying the idealized *ejidal* model of social relations and power structures presented by Redfield to the more realistic model Goldkind proposes. Redfield's homogeneous society is similar in every way to the assumptions made by the agency funding the CBT project about the social structure of the village of Ek'Balam, whereas the actual situation found eight years after the opening of the Cabañas follows Goldkind's reinterpretation of the data. Based on the differences in participation levels shown in figure 5.2, a few kin groups dominate the CBT project and receive the majority of the benefit. This is not the outcome imagined by the CDI, and Ek'Balam is not the homogeneous, idyllic "little community" that was to be the foundation for this project. From the outside, residents of Ek'Balam appear to be in similar social and economic situations. In comparison to the places from which most visitors, volunteers, and project staff come, this is a poor village. What they do not see initially is that within this level of poverty are many levels of relative poverty. The differences are invisible in this and other, similar development contexts, which means that the important nuances are overlooked.

Levels of participation in Ek'Balam's CBT project are one way by which we can identify the differences between kin groups. Participation in the political life of the village is another useful area to examine. Figure 5.5 shows the number of years someone from each of the kin groups served as municipal commissioner (mayor) in Ek'Balam since the move from X'Kumil in 1971.

With the exception of the first term, which was served by a member of the Dzib kin group, and the second term, served by a member of the Mena kin group, all municipal authorities are members of the Ay, Chan, or May kin groups. These same three groups have the highest levels of participation in the CBT project and are generally the most financially secure and politically powerful kin groups in the village. This does not imply that they are wealthy, only that they have higher levels of household income than the other kin groups.

The domination of community-based projects by elites is especially common in rural areas. Mansuri and Rao (2007) attribute this to the power held by village elites based on their ability to speak with development planners, read project documents, and manage finances. The role of external institutions can exacerbate the elite domination of a project. According to Clark Jackson (1997), this happens when the institution's frontline staff overlooks local power relations because of the pressure to report positive results. In addition, there is rarely interaction between the agents of the institution and any locals other than those representing the project's leadership; therefore, agency representatives are not aware of the perception of the project by the community at large. When staff members from the funding agency come to Ek'Balam, they, too, deal exclusively with the project leaders. They are understandably eager to see it succeed and do not question the actual effects of the project or the sharing of benefits throughout the community.

These conclusions follow those of many other social scientists working with community-based development projects, both in and out of the realm of tourism. The existing social relationships and power structures contained within "the Community" are exactly why the use of this term as a defining category over which development initiatives can be superimposed is so troublesome. In Ek'Balam as in most small, rural, indigenous communities presented as case studies in the literature, the rhetoric of benefits shared among the community can be realized as a reality only when the development trajectory is slow, focused, and based in careful use of existing local knowledge.

Maya Cosmopolitans

Residents of Ek'Balam know that tourists do not come all the way to this small village only to see blenders, T-shirts emblazoned with sports team logos, and other signposts of all things modern. These items are not of great interest in and of themselves. For years travelers—be they tourists, anthropologists, or otherwise—have sought the experience of the "Other." What is of interest, however, is the level of cognition the "Other" has of this phenomenon. Multiple strategies are employed at the household level to perform tourism (Little 2004b, 2000; Edensor 2001; Kirshenblatt-Gimblett 1998; Annis 1987), and residents view having this knowledge as simply good business sense. Clearly, if someone is paying for a tour of a Mayan home, you need to provide exactly that. It is here that the ideas of modernity, authenticity, tradition, and cosmopolitanism become fluid and difficult to identify as discrete characteristics within an individual and a community.

This chapter takes as its point of departure Ferguson and Gupta's (2002, 981) discussion of the shifting role of the state in shaping "local communities." This is based in part on the realization that states are not simply "functional bureaucratic apparatuses, but powerful sites of symbolic and cultural production that

DOI: 10.5876/9781607327721.c006

are themselves always culturally represented and understood in particular ways" (Ferguson and Gupta 2002, 981). This production of cultural symbols makes the state socially effective. These concepts are particularly useful in understanding what I have come to refer to as "government-sponsored Maya-ness."

Ferguson and Gupta, following Michel Foucault (1991), discuss the concepts of verticality and encompassment in the context of the new wave of non-governmental organizations (NGOs) as purveyors of development. This is an apt lens with which to examine the situation in Yucatán, where in many cases the state itself, which has historically been the top in "top-down" development, is instituting community-based tourism (CBT) projects. This shifts the approach on the part of the state, but the effect on the actual projects and the communities charged with managing them remains unclear. What we find is a situation in which the local is the symbolic seat of power in the project, but the state is still guiding the cultural production aspect to maintain its social effectiveness.

SUMMER 2010

This summer afternoon finds us all enjoying the late afternoon breeze under the Almendra tree at the Ay Mena house. Rosa and Modesto's baby, the first grandchild, is being passed around among his uncles, his grandfather, and his aunt Vanessa. This child is at the center of all activities and has alleviated the remaining hostility after the couple eloped last spring. His four uncles call him the "fifth brother," and everyone agrees that he is the new king of the household. Vanessa has taken an active role with Cristian and spends much of her time caring for him. Many residents remark that she is gifted when it comes to childcare. What started last year as a subtle interest in continuing her studies is now blossoming as she realizes the potential to study to become a midwife. Midwives are rare these days, and a majority of women go to the hospital to give birth.

Salvador is eighteen and reconsidering his educational options. Since he left school last year to start working on the coast, things have begun to pick back up in the village's growing tourism economy. He just found out about an opportunity that may help him fulfill his dream of being able to stay in the village instead of working in Cancún. A new program just started that will give him the opportunity to train as a guide at the archaeological zone. He is uncertain of whether he should sign up for the program, though, because it will be a larger burden on his family's finances. The classes are held periodically in Mérida, which means he will have to pay for transportation and lodging while staying there. This is a great opportunity for him, though, one that will not come again.

Life in Cancún this past year was hard on Salvador, but his characteristically calm demeanor has not left him. Eugenio, in contrast, feels he has been working in Cancún too long to stop now. He is accustomed to his life there and to the income he brings in. He speaks wistfully about living full-time in Ek'Balam some-day, but it seems unlikely to him that he would be able to make a living there.

A heavy silence punctuates discussions about the young men who are migrating. Just two months ago Antonio, a young man from Ek'Balam, died while incarcerated in Cancún. The village is still reeling from this news. He was working on a construction crew, but there was not enough work to keep all the workers. His boss hired him out to another man who had work. His new job was to guard a junk lot on the outskirts of the city. By day, Antonio was stripping the items of any valuable metals, and by night, he was to sleep there and make sure that no one else was coming into the lot to do the same. The job was good for a few weeks, but then the boss stopped coming as fre-quently. He owed Antonio two weeks' pay when he came again. The boss did not have the money and left without paying him. The next time he came, Antonio explained that he was nearly out of food and water and did not have any money to buy more. The man said he would be back in two days with his pay. A week later, Antonio still had not seen his boss. He had not eaten and was rationing the little water he had. He decided that he needed to do some-thing or he would die there.

Antonio took some of the copper he had stripped and set off to sell it. The boss returned the next day and filed a report that Antonio had stolen from him. He was incarcerated immediately. Baltazar, Lucas and Gomercinda's nephew, was the supervisor of the crew Antonio was on before being hired out to this other job. When he was allowed to make a phone call, he contacted Baltazar to tell him what had happened and ask him to post bail. Baltazar did not have the money, but he contacted his employer hoping that he would. The employer responded that this was not his problem, since Antonio was no longer his employee. Eight days later Baltazar received another call from jail; it was an officer with news that Antonio was dead. He asked Baltazar to contact his family and to come get his personal effects. Eugenio talks very little about this incident but says he thinks about it constantly. His parents worry about him even more now because he is drinking more and more. They fear that one day he will be the one who does not come home.

The younger boys are fourteen and fifteen and continue to grow in oppo-site directions while remaining best friends. Federico cannot spend enough time with the volunteers. He is with them now, at "the party" in the center of town each summer. Nacho is still uninterested, though his desire to finish school as soon as possible is changing. He thought he would leave after the sixth grade, but he will graduate this summer and has decided to continue at the junior high in the neighboring town of Actuncóh. I asked him about this change of heart and he explained that with all the changes going on in the *ejido*, he wants to be educated enough to protect their land. "Knowledge about making milpa isn't enough these days," he says. He wants to have an education so that if the family does fall on hard times, selling their land will never be the only option.

Vanessa is twelve this summer and spends the time when she is not helping with Cristian working with the volunteers on the community museum project. The goal is to create a museum in the multipurpose room at the CBT project. The museum will be a traditional Maya house and kitchen and will incorporate all of the authentic items found in a Maya home. To accomplish this, volunteers have been running around the village over the last week asking residents to donate items from their homes. Once everything has been gathered, signage in the museum will identify and describe each item. This is an ambitious plan, but residents are engaging with the museum project in ways they have not engaged with the volunteers in summers past. While the concept of the community museum was designed and introduced by the volunteer organization, residents are taking a major role in changing it and shaping the outcomes. The museum was not envisioned as particularly historical in nature; however, when they started collecting items for the museum, a few older residents participating in the CBT project decided that the history of Ek'Balam needed to be included. Much talk centered on their arrival story, a central piece of the historical narrative in Ek'Balam.

The interactions surrounding the museum mark the first time the relationship between history and authenticity has really been debated in the context of the CBT project. There is strong disagreement about what should be included in the museum to represent a traditional Maya home. Some men feel there should be metal pots and utensils, iron hooks, and dishes. They argue that the only modern objects that should be excluded are items made of plastic, which would date the traditional home to approximately the 1960s. Others argue that the home should be "more authentic." They feel it should not have metal pots and hooks and should be appointed in the way of the *antiguos* (ancient ones), which broadly refers to those who were alive when the monuments were constructed, before the Spaniards came. This group wants to see a hammock woven of sisal in the museum because the colored nylon thread used today would not have been available then. The most interesting aspect of this process is the diachronic nature of the plans for authenticity. Potential "present day" for the museum could be at the time when the monuments were occupied, in the sixteenth-century settlement of Tiquibalon, or during the hacienda era. After substantial deliberation, participants determined that the museum should represent a house from the beginning of Ek'Balam's current occupation. This would be around 1965–75, when they began to build up the town in its present location.

Both doña Gomercinda and don Lucas are interested in the museum and have been sending various household items with Vanessa to donate to the project. Lucas and Nacho even completed a *xux* (large basket for harvesting corn) for the museum yesterday, which is about the most involvement in the volunteer projects Nacho is interested in having. Eugenio and Modesto break in to our conversation about the community museum with their own concerns about doing all this work for tourists, whose spending will not benefit everyone in the community. Participation in the CBT project has dwindled even more over the last year, in part because of concerns that tourism would never recover from the Swine Flu scare. 'Genio continues to question his father's dedication to the project. If it were up to him, their family would have left the project years ago. Modesto's family left the project in the early years, and his input strengthens 'Genio's concerns. For Lucas and Goma, membership as associates in the CBT project is an investment they are sure will pay off. They say they do not really care about the question of authentic or inauthentic Maya culture. Lucas says, "I know who I am, and if who I am is interesting to a gringo and they want to come learn more about me and my family . . . welcome."

AUTHENTIC MAYAS

Yucatán's tourism promotion agency, Secretaria de Turismo del Estado de Yucatán (SECATUR-Yucatán), relies heavily on the popularity of archaeological zones and Maya culture in its promotions. Governmental and non-governmental agencies communicate the importance of satisfying the tourist gaze to residents of Ek'Balam in multiple ways, including interactions through the village tour and strong suggestions from the main agency sponsoring the community tourism project (the National Commission for the Development of Indigenous Villages [CDI]) regarding the presentation of Mayan culture through employee dress codes and staged ritual ceremonies. This marketing strategy by the government and tourism industry has elicited an interesting response among residents of Ek'Balam. In a manner similar to what Walter E. Little (2004a) found in his work in Aguas Calientes, Guatemala, rather than dismiss tourists' interest in their lifestyle, residents have embraced their notoriety and are engaged in a near-constant performance of tourism.

John Urry (1990) introduced the concept of the "tourist gaze" to the field of tourism studies, and it has greatly influenced subsequent studies (Perkins and Thorns 2001). Urry defined this idea as a departure from Foucault's "medical gaze" as presented in *The Birth of the Clinic* (Foucault 2003). According to Urry, the tourist experience is created in large part by gazing at environments that are somehow different from those found in tourists' everyday surroundings. If touring is a process of gazing at whatever is encountered, then the construction of these encounters is the defining force underlying what (or who) is the recipient of the tourist gaze (Urry 1990, 1). The idea of individuals residing in a tourism destination as passive subjects of a tourist's gaze assumes that these individuals have neither agency in the process nor cognition of their role. Because we know this assumption to be false, the concept of the engaged performance of tourism as the response to the gaze is more useful.

Increasing numbers of scholars discuss the concept of performing tourism. Little (2004a) focused on the public performances for tourists in Guatemalan marketplaces and found them to be much more than sales strategies. He refers to the process of residents building rapport with tourists for the purpose of making a sale as performance, in part because they are not building long-term relationships and the encounters are therefore temporary (Little 2004a, 530). Tim Edensor (2001) looks to Erving Goffman's (1999) discussion of the roles we play in everyday life in both the "front stage" and the "backstage." He explains this dichotomy as follows: "The nature of the tourist stage contextualizes performance: whether it is carefully managed, facilitates transit and contains discretely situated objects (props); or whether its boundaries are blurred, [and] it is cluttered with other actors playing different roles" (Edensor 2001, 63).

From this description of the process, we can see that the "actors" are not just performing tourism but are also performing "otherness." To further the metaphor, let us look to Disneyland as a destination. All employees there are "cast members" and as such are in a state of constant performance, from the moment they step through the door in the tall wall that separates the theme park (front stage) from the outside world (backstage) until they leave for the day. Their expressions, costumes, and often even mannerisms correspond to the particular "land" in which they work. It would be jarring to see a pirate in Tomorrowland, for example. This, according to Mike Crang (1997), is but one example of the "meaningful settings that tourists consume and tourism employees help produce" (Edensor 2001 cf. Crang 1997, 69). When applied to the situation in Ek'Balam, the residents are the "cast members" and the places in and on which the tourists rest their gaze comprise the "front stage." The implications for these encounters are many, but it is when the lines between "front stage" and "backstage" are blurred that they become problematic.

The village tour offered through a hotel in Ek'Balam is a popular activity that many guests say is the highlight of their vacation. The tour consists of visits to three houses in the village to see different women performing daily tasks. At doña Gomercinda's house, guests learn how she prepares the corn and grinds it on the *metate*. They are then able to try their hands at tortilla making and eat fresh, hot tortillas before moving on to the next stop. From doña Gomercinda's house the tour moves on the house of doña Ana, where visitors can watch her embroider the traditional *huipil* (shift dress made of white cotton, with floral embroidery at the collar and hem) still worn by a few women, children's dresses, and napkin sets on her treadle sewing machine. The last stop on the tour is the house of doña Gloria, who gives an impromptu weaving demonstration and lets visitors attempt to weave a few rows of the hammock on her loom.

Doña Gomercinda's house is a favorite stop on the tour because of the high level of interaction involved in the tortilla-making demonstration. Guests are fascinated by the *metate* she uses to grind her corn and are amazed when they attempt to do so and realize the amount of strength it takes. They inevitably ask how much corn she grinds each day and how long it takes her. With a twinkle in her eye, she explains that grinding enough corn for the 400 or so tortillas consumed daily by her family of eight takes about four hours on the *metate*. By this time the muscles in the visitors' arms are aching and they may have pinched a finger or two between the stones, but they never turn around to see the metal hand crank secured to one wall of the kitchen house and wonder how much more efficient that tool would be. The *metate* belonged to doña Gomercinda's great-grandparents, and she says she remembers her mother using it from time to time, but she has never once ground corn on it for anything other than this tour. When the visitors move on, she will wash the *metate* and return it to the corner of the kitchen where it will stay until the next tour comes through, after which she will grind the day's corn in the shiny metal grinder that is one of her most prized possessions.

The example of doña Gomercinda's tortilla-making performance would fall squarely into Dean MacCannell's (1976, 91) conception of "staged authenticity." He argues that encounters such as this contain "a kind of strained truthfulness [that] is similar in most of its particulars to a little lie" and that "social structure itself is involved in the construction of the type of mystification that supports social reality" (MacCannell 1976, 93). If this "mystification" is deliberate, then one must recognize the role the "cast member" (doña Gomercinda in this case) plays in the process. Knowledge of what the tourist expects to see and experience in this encounter is required to successfully set the stage and provide an adequate feeling of authenticity, thus making her possession of this intercultural awareness a display of her cosmopolitanism.

To discuss ideas such as cosmopolitanism in the context presented here, it is important to begin by identifying definitions of this concept. Sheldon Pollock and colleagues (2000) define cosmopolitanism as much as they define its opposite; that is, they tell us what it is not: it is not a known entity to be traced from the Stoics through Kant as attempted by David B. Harvey (2000), nor is it a concept that has been fully realized. What it is, according to Pollock and colleagues (2000, 577), is something that has an inherent need to remain undefined because "specifying cosmopolitanism positively and definitely is an uncosmopolitan thing to do." One solid place on which to stand is the fact that social, cultural, and historic forces such as nationalism, globalization, and translocation are managed by the adaptive strategy of cosmopolitanism.

Ulf Hannerz (1990, 239) defines the concept loosely as simply people who move about in the world; however, in a stricter sense he sees it as the "coexistence of cultures in the individual experience." The context of a rural village in the midst of tourism development offers an interesting dynamic to his discussion of what it means to be cosmopolitan. Given the tone and trajectory of Hannerz's article, he was speaking about Western travelers and even made the distinction between the cosmopolitan and the more pedestrian "tourist," with whom cosmopolitans abhor being confused. Yet he goes on to discuss cosmopolitanism as more than a state of being but also as a competence achieved by an individual. He describes this competence as "a personal ability to make one's way into other cultures, through listening, looking, intuiting, and reflecting" (Hannerz 1990, 242). In essence, Hannerz (1990, 243) is defining cosmopolitanism as a state of awareness of and engagement with the "Other" vis-à-vis a constant maneuvering through "a particular system of meanings and meaningful forms." Therefore, I argue that cosmopolitanism as an adaptive strategy is employed at the local level not by tourists hoping to be redefined as sophisticated travelers through interaction with the "Other-Maya" but by residents of Ek'Balam (re)defining themselves as sufficiently "Maya" for consumption by the "Other-tourist." Further, the exercise of cosmopolitanism as an adaptation is a tactic used by residents to maintain engagement with the state for continued support of their community-based tourism project while concurrently yielding to the state's strategies for touristic performance. Importantly, this redefinition of Maya-ness is not solely for external consumption. Rather, residents are simultaneously involved in an internal process that redefines their own perceptions of connections between themselves and the ancient inhabitants of the area (Ardren 2002; Alonso Olvera 2015).

"... IT WASN'T VERY MAYA"

To understand how cosmopolitanism plays out in touristic encounters at the local level, I would like to offer an ethnographic example from Ek'Balam. In the summer of 2004 I asked don Felipe, one of the men running the community-based tourism project, about their plans to cater to tourists and what sorts of things the community hoped to offer:

> It would be best if we could have some activities in the afternoons, like walks with [tourists] through the jungle to teach them what we know. We could organize a *hetz-mek*, it is a ritual we do when a boy is four months old. We do it because when he grows he will work the milpa, which has four corners. For girls it is at three months, like the three stones around the fire. The tourists are all very interested in things like this. We could also have a Ch'a Chaak so that they can see how we care for our milpas. The INI [CDI] tells us that this will bring more guests here because there are not many places that still have their traditions where the tourists can go to see things like this. It would be good if we could organize things like this for the visitor to see. ~Don Felipe [Transcriptions 2004-0617]

This aspect of performance for tourists is found in other parts of life in the village as well, including traditional rituals and ceremonies. Not long after my arrival in Ek'Balam in 2004, I was invited to the annual Ch'a Chaak (rain-calling) ceremony. Chaak, the god of rain, is the patron of this event. However, he shares the day with the Virgin Mary.

The Ch'a Chaak ceremony takes place in the middle of *la canícula*, a period of drought before the heavy rains, which usually lasts from the middle of June through the middle of July. This is an especially crucial time for the residents of Ek'Balam who are still farming; the corn has been planted and is growing but remains small and vulnerable to a severe lack of water. The eventual yield of the milpa depends on the rains coming before the ground has dried completely. For this reason, it is necessary to hold the Ch'a Chaak sometime in the first two weeks of July.

Two groups are involved in the preparation and execution of this important ceremony: the men who run the ceremony and their wives. One *ejidatario* is designated as the *dueño*, or sponsor, of the ceremony. This is a large financial commitment, as it is his responsibility to provide the cleared land on which the ceremony is held and to pay the *hmeen*, or Maya priest. Each man who participates must be able to bring *masa* (the ground corn used to make tortillas) and a chicken as offerings to Chaak. The *dueño* of the ceremony in 2004 was don Lucas, the father of the Ay Mena family.

The ceremony began at 7:00 a.m. with the making of the sacred wine and the construction of the altar. The *yax mesa*, or green table, is at the center of this and many other Mayan rituals. Made of a table with four intersecting arches in the cardinal directions, it represents a portal between earth and sky through which the various gods can be contacted. Juan de la Cruz Pech was the *hmeen* who ran the ceremony, and he welcomed me when I arrived. Between each of the four phases of the ceremony, he stopped to explain some of what they were doing, as everything was carried out in Maya and in 2004 I knew approximately five words in that language.

After the ceremony, I had many questions as to the way this ceremony has changed over the years. Though I was familiar with some of the central aspects of the ceremony, such as the construction of the *yax mesa*, I had expected to see the majority of the male residents who were still farming in attendance, save for the handful of Seventh Day Adventists. Once the day got under way, however, I realized that only nine men were participating this year. I later inquired about this in a conversation with don Rafael. He explained that many of the religious ceremonies are lacking in attendance, if they are held at all:

There are changes in the faith of people here. Before, all believed in the ceremonies. Now there are many religions and it is like politics. Before this time of rain

the people said, "we need the rain," now it has come to grow their milpas. They say, "Thank God," but who among them was there at the Ch'a Chaak? God sent the rain because we asked for it. We spoke the name of Chaak. There are almost no people who still believe, they think they can speak directly to God. The ceremony that we had 15 days ago celebrates being Maya. There is another ceremony called lo-ca-pal. It is a new benediction for the land. You do it for the milpa too. We do it every two years to renew the land and the animals. Usually it is about 20 people. But now, no. The last time we had this was 4 years ago. They are going to be lost, because how will the children know about them. There are many changes.
~Don Rafael [Transcriptions 2007-0718 (01:12:47)]

In the summer of 2007, I expected to attend the ceremony again and was interested to see how the levels of participation had changed over the three years since my first stay. In the month of June, I began to inquire about the date the Ch'a Chaak would take place. Each of the individuals I spoke with was hesitant to give me a time and instead told me to ask someone else. By July there was little pretense about holding the ceremony at all, and I was told that there would be no Ch'a Chaak this year. According to many residents, this was the first time a summer passed without this important event.

Similar to the encounter at the house of doña Gomercinda discussed earlier, these conversations with don Felipe reveal a person who is completely aware of tourists' expectations and desires and is able to cater to them through the selective presentation of "traditional" rituals. At the same time, he recognizes the importance of demonstrating this competency to the CDI without letting it come through in the performance for tourists. To accomplish this, he and other residents employ the tactics at their disposal. These tactics are informed by the daily tourist discourse about what they expect to see, desire to experience, and do not want to know.

In the summer of 2010, a Ch'a Chaak ceremony was again held in a clearing on the outskirts of the village. The following is an ethnographic account of this event and an analysis of what it illuminates with regard to understanding touristic performance and cosmopolitanism. The scene is a clearing in the woods on the outskirts of a small Maya village. There is a hmeen in the center of the clearing whispering an eclectic mix of prayers to Ch'a Chaak, Jesus, and Maria. He kneels at a table made of leaves and branches that is the altar for many Maya rituals. The yax mesa has leafy branches that arch over it and attach to each corner, resembling the arch of the sky and the celestial realm. Surrounding him are chickens that have recently died, an aluminum tub of wine made from the Balche tree, and buckets of masa. There are jicaras made of small dried gourds that will be used to drink the sweet corn atole that accompanies special occasions like this.

The importance of the ceremony and the role of the h-men have been well documented by generations of anthropologists in the region, and as an ethnographer I am quite taken by this scene. This was previously an annual event, but as a result of many changes within the community, the last time the village held a Ch'a Chaak ceremony was during my first summer there in 2004. The experience of being invited to observe something I had heard of through the pages of ethnographies by the likes of Redfield and others was amazing to me. I was, admittedly, a tourist of sorts. A guest among hosts, an "anthropologist-Other." I suppose that they could have done anything and I would have thought that, regardless of what I expected, it was very "Maya."

Returning to 2010, let us redirect our gaze from the center of the clearing to the edges. Standing, sitting, mingling, and crouching to get the best view are approximately sixty people consisting of tourists, volunteers, project staff from a federal development agency, state and local politicians, representatives from the state secretary of tourism, and me, the "anthropologist-Other." What we are witnessing is an event co-sponsored and organized by the Conservation Corps of Yucatán (CCY, an NGO), the CDI, and members of the civil association in the village that manages a community-based tourism project. The volunteers had spent the last month working on various development projects in the village through the CCY program. The politicians were invited by SECATUR to see how regional community-based tourism projects are run. The tourists were simply guests staying at the community-run hotel, fortunate to have arrived when they did.

The strobing of sixty flashbulbs lights the scene, and excitement is radiating from the crowd. I am thinking that this is going quite well and that the various delegates will be very pleased. This sentiment is shared by the president of the civic association, who thinks they have really nailed what was requested: a traditional Maya rain ceremony. The women in the kitchen cleaning and cooking the chickens killed during the ceremony feel the same. They tell me that the old tradition was to have the Ch'a Chaak overnight, lasting from about 10:00 p.m. until dawn the next morning. It had been many years since they had done one like that, but for this occasion they wanted to demonstrate the most authentic rain ceremony they could.

The Ch'a Chaak ceremony ended at dawn, and everyone returned to their hammocks to rest before starting the day. As I walked home with the family I stay with, we discussed the level of Maya-ness displayed, and they explained how hard it had been to find a *hmeen* who would still perform an overnight ceremony. When I asked again why they wanted it to be held overnight, they said the guests in attendance were very important to the continued funding of U Najil Ek'Balam, the community-based tourism project in the village, and that they were clear about wanting this event to be *maya verdadero* (real Maya).

Once we arrived at the Ay Mena house, I asked what "real" Maya was. Doña Goma said that one way to tell a real Maya is from the person's attire but then noted that if that were the case, then she would not be Maya because she dresses in a modern style of skirts and dresses instead of a *huipil*. Vanessa, the youngest daughter, added that she thought Maya meant both being a mestiza (a woman who still wears a *huipil* daily) and speaking Maya. Goma quickly saw the contradiction in this and exclaimed that if she made me a *huipil* to wear, then I would be a *sak maya* (white Maya) and if she learned English, then she would be a *box gringa* (black or dark North American woman). We continued joking about how the women politicians who attended the ceremony wore beautiful *ternos*, the dress version of the traditional *huipil*, and the actual Maya women did not because they spent the ceremony working in the kitchen. A simple *huipil* can cost upward of 500 pesos (US$50) because of the detailed embroidery. For most women, this is not the preferred attire for killing and cleaning chickens. I asked Vanessa how we could identify a man as Maya or not, and she explained that a man would be whatever his wife was. At this Nacho, one of the family's sons, ran out of the kitchen house and returned promptly with his father's machete tied to his waist with a rope and his T-shirt turned inside out to hide the Los Angeles Angels logo. He pounded his chest with his fist and said in his deepest voice, "*soy maya* (I am Maya)."

We found out the next day that we were not the only ones who noticed these paradoxes. The final word from the esteemed attendees at the ceremony was not as positive as expected. They wanted to know why none of the women in their beautiful *huipiles* were at the ceremony and why the women in the kitchen were not wearing their "Maya dresses" while they worked. They were dismayed at having to stay up all night to see the whole ceremony, and the ones who returned to their rooms for a few hours of sleep during the night were frustrated at having missed part of the ceremony. In parting, the politicians thanked the leaders of the civil association for their trouble and stated that while the event had gone smoothly, "it wasn't very Maya" (Fieldnotes: 2009–0724).

This episode illustrates some of the disparate logics within which residents of Ek'Balam negotiate tourism and conduct their daily lives. Households in this community balance economic strategies that prioritize tourism with traditional economic strategies for land use and are all the while reminded that they should maintain a sufficiently "Maya" identity regardless of how the balance tips. Among the economic strategies that prioritize tourism are handicraft production, biodiversity conservation, and the provision of accommodations and other touristic services. Traditional strategies for land use are mainly milpa agriculture, producing maize for auto-consumption. This balancing act reinforces the idea that tourism is the new game in town, and as milpa agriculture decreases, some worry that it will soon be the only game in town. From the development agency's point of view, this is positive; this is progress. Subsistence agriculture is not rational from a neo-liberal economic standpoint. What we see repeating here in the relations between state agencies and residents of indigenous communities is the classic "economic man" discussion laid out by Frank Cancian. He asks, "Are peasants able to be economic maximizers or are they unable to maximize because they are bound to traditional production strategies" (Cancian 1972, 1)? This question has been posed, answered, re-phrased, and even discarded; however, we have not actually moved as far from it as we would like to believe. Guillermo de la Peña (1982) questions some of the models of modernization, unilineal change, and the peasantry that have been presented with regard to this issue. He argues that "the national economy—more precisely, the process of capital accumulation—has entailed the existence of 'non-modern' sectors, articulated to 'modern' organizations" (de la Peña 1982, 26). It is at this juncture that touristic performance, as a means to capital accumulation, becomes a form of governmentality.

TACTICS AND STRATEGIES OF GOVERNMENTALITY

Foucault defined governmentality as "how people govern themselves and others through the production and reproduction of knowledge" (quoted in Wearing and McDonald 2002, 197). While the use of the concept by James Ferguson and Akhil Gupta (2002, 989) remains similar, they posit governmentality in the shifting context of the neo-liberal economic project to develop their idea of transnational governmentality. In Ek'Balam, governmentality can be seen as enacted on two levels: residents distribute knowledge and how to best exploit the presence of tourists in their village by producing adequate levels of Maya-ness, and the funding agency, working on behalf of the federal government, governs residents by mandating the display of their Maya-ness for tourist consumption.

The shift by the state from a position of verticality to one of encompassment, as both the top and bottom of development through the creation of agencies such as the CDI, allows it to enact a different kind of governmentality. To be successful at gaining and maintaining funding, residents are expected to respond to this shift in multiple ways. However, their funding is on the line and they have little power over the way they are governed through their tourism project, leaving them with only the tactic of being un-cosmopolitan cosmopolitans.

For Michel de Certeau, the difference between strategy and tactic lies in power. He defines a strategy as "the calculation (or manipulation) of power relationships" when a subject has a "base from which relations can be managed" (De Certeau 1984, 35). In contrast, a tactic is "a calculated action determined by the absence of a proper locus" (De Certeau 1984, 37). Those using tactics must act within boundaries delimited either by the law or by a foreign power. In addition, those using tactics do not have the advantage of viewing their "adversary as a whole within a distinct, visible, and objectifiable space" (de Certeau 1984, 37). This is a useful lens through which the daily negotiations with tourism in Ek'Balam can be viewed and understood.

This discussion of cosmopolitanism, performance, and governmentality in the context of rural tourism development provides ethnographic evidence that frames negotiations with tourism and touristic performance. As previously discussed, they occupy a space between cosmopolitan and indigenous, tradition and modernity, in which they must cater to very different demands of both. Residents are constantly producing and reproducing their identity as Maya and indigenous while flexing their knowledge of touristic desires and good business sense to create and maintain successful engagement with the tourism industry. Following Veena Das and Deborah Poole's (2004) discussion of the margins of the state, I argue that the foray of the Mexican state into the business of indigenous development effectively blurred these lines and created a model that is found in many similar contexts outside of Ek'Balam and even outside Mexico. The movement of the government to an encompassment model complicates its interactions with residents and blurs the expectations it has for the projects it funds. Moving fluidly between a hands-off "if you build it they will come" form of governmentality and a high-involvement directive to "be as Maya as you can be" is but one of the strategies government funders possess. The response to these strategies at the local level, as we have seen through the examples provided here, has been the creation and employment of the multiple tactics necessary to perform tourism.

Defining Successful Community Development

Measuring success in community-based tourism (CBT) is difficult because the triple bottom line (TBL) often does not include realistic metrics for social cohesion or social capital. Attempts at measuring the success of CBT endeavors vary in their feasibility and ultimate utility. This common difficulty has been discussed in the literature since the rise of alternative and sustainable tourism development (Okazaki 2008; Stonich 2005; Wearing and McDonald 2002). Similarly, the discourse of sustainability often provides a contradictory argument to development scenarios focused on conserving and maintaining cultural heritage (Barthel-Bouchier 2016). Indigenous tourism development adds another layer of difficulty to the assessment process because of the small scale of most indigenous tourism projects and numerous other issues (see Carr, Ruhanen, and Whitford 2016). Part of the problem lies in the TBL metric used to assess existing and potential projects. This metric accounts for ecological health, financial sustainability, and local social capital; however, it does not account for local differences in defining a successful project or variations in access to capital within the community.

DOI: 10.5876/9781607327721.c007

The concept of social capital has been presented as the missing link between successful economic development and approaches to projects that will be locally sustainable. Social capital has recently become a presence in discussions of development (Grootaert and Van Bastelaer 2002). This term refers to the quantitative and qualitative nature of social relations and gives value to existing social networks that can be used to create collaboration to achieve the common goal as defined by the actors in a given social group (Jones 2005, 305). Because of the exogenous nature of most tourism projects, "local people and their communities have become the objects of development, but not the subjects of it" (Mitchell and Reid 2001, 114). Participatory development strategies attempt to create a reverse development environment by working from initiatives identified and defined within the community. Social capital is a link between the theoretical benefits of participation and the actual success of the community-based approach, and it is necessary for viable tourism development projects. High levels of social capital can alleviate some of the pertinent issues, such as the definition of community and levels of cooperation. Communities with high social capital are more clearly defined and demonstrate increased agreement on this definition; however, few methodologies have been developed for the measurement of this phenomenon, and it is therefore suspect to critics of participatory development (Fine 2001).

Drastic variations in access to this project and its benefits could indicate that the project was a failure in terms of its goal of strengthening social capital. Conversely, the income improvements and ever-growing list of content customers in the project's first decade are interpreted as successes from a financial perspective. Understanding the variations between bridging and bonding social capital enables us to differentiate between direct and indirect benefits from tourism through the CBT project. Bonding social capital was not strengthened within the community. The existing ties of more powerful kin groups were potentially strengthened through the process; however, the kin groups that did not participate in the CBT project experienced no bonding with the local elite groups. The same is true for kin groups whose members began participating and subsequently left the project. The tension generated by this process further degraded these relationships.

The strengthening of bridging social capital is evident in the establishment of connections between residents participating in the project and external groups. Interestingly, bridging social capital can communicate a false positive to project planners in terms of successful project outcomes. They often treat the community as one homogeneous group and work with specific individuals. For the families involved in the project at this level, new positive connections have been made. This bridging social capital brings an array of indirect benefits that are not immediately apparent. In this final visit with the Ay Mena family on an evening in January 2012, we learn more about the ways they have weathered the process of tourism development in their community. Their story provides an example of the indirect benefits of tourism development seen throughout the village.

WINTER 2012

The first days of the New Year are the *xok k'in* (counting days), which predict the weather for the rest of the year. Each day from January 1 through January 12 represents a month, counting forward from January 1. January 13 through 24 represent the months in reverse order. Each of the six days between January 25 and 30 represents two days, and January 31 is the *gran final* (big finish); every hour beginning at 12:00 a.m. represents a month, first counting forward to 11:59 a.m., then backward from noon to 11:59 p.m. The ability to predict the weather is important here, as it is for any farmer. The men carefully observe the weather during the month and discuss it at length in the evenings in conversations on the plaza and around the dinner table.

Don Lucas spends much of the time during dinner this evening going over the weather patterns of the first part of the *xok k'in* with his four sons and his son-in-law. They have been out to the milpas nearly every day for the last week. Lucas says he needs to see how much rain falls on his fields because sometimes the amount of rain there differs from that in the village. Modesto, Rosas's husband, agrees and asks how the rainfall has been on Lucas's milpa. He is working both his father's and his brothers' milpas, which are in very different parts of the *ejido* from Lucas's parcel. Rosa and Modesto "escaped" (eloped) in June 2009. She is now twenty and has recently given birth to their second child, Maria. During the first part of their relationship, they lived with his family just down the street, as is customary. Ever since Maria was born, they have been living at the Ay Mena house, and they show no signs of leaving. The family has accepted Modesto for the most part, although Eugenio still tries to rile him up when they are drinking.

Eugenio joins the conversation with questions about how much is left in the fields to harvest. Eugenio moved home from Cancún in September. He said there was very little work there and he missed his family. Some work became available at the archaeological zone replacing the huge *palapa* that covers the stuccoes, so he was happy to take it. The family is large now and has spread out to fill all the houses. After the hurricanes in 2005, the government program CONAVIT brought cinderblock houses to Ek'Balam and most other villages in the region. They finished the construction of their cinderblock house in 2006, but it remained mostly empty until 2009, when they finished the concrete floor and the stucco in the walls. Now, both the blockhouse and the thatch house are full. The kitchen is jam-packed with Goma and Lucas; Rosa, Modesto, and their two babies; the four boys; Vanessa, and me. We eat in waves, with each one vacating the table when he or she finishes. Vanessa fills bowls and makes sure there are enough tortillas on the table.

Federico and Salvador sit side by side and periodically burst into laughter. They are half-listening to the conversation about the recent weather and half-exchanging insults with each other. Federico is still in school and is as suave as ever. He loves to sing and desperately wants to learn how to play the guitar. He is convinced that being a musician is the way to a girl's heart. His preoccupation with girls at age seventeen is normal, but Goma still worries that he is going to run off or "get into trouble" with one of the volunteers with whom he is frequently spending time. When the volunteers come either in large groups or individually through one of the volunteer programs, they work with the children of the CBT project's associates on whatever project they are assigned. Lucas is one of the eleven remaining associates, so his sons are often invited to work with the volunteers. Federico jumps at these opportunities and talks to me at length about how smart and pretty the female volunteers are. Unfortunately, these interactions have also left some young men with irreparably marred reputations. The volunteers go home, but the young men who were seen spending so much time with them are deemed unfit for local girls to date and potentially marry. This situation has damaged relationships between some families as well. When a girl's parents deny a young man the privilege of visiting their daughter, his family often takes great offense because it is a reflection on how they raised their son. Luckily, Federico has not gained this reputation, but he tells me it is only a matter of time.

In contrast, Nacho has no interest in the volunteers or the CBT project in general. Both he and Eugenio encourage Lucas to quit the project because they think it is a waste of effort and resources. At sixteen, Nacho still spends his days going to school, helping his father in the fields, and improving his aim with the slingshot. He is still gruff and is much more serious than his brothers are. He does not care for dressing up and refuses to use the hair gel from the big tub his brothers use daily. He says that when he is in the forest, it does not matter what he looks like, and that is where he wants to spend his days. The times he softens up are when he is playing with his niece and nephew, Maria and Cristian.

Vanessa has made sure that everyone has enough to eat and is now back to taking care of Cristian. His uncles were feeding him but have announced that he is a disaster and are happy to give the job back to their youngest sister. Vanessa is a young woman now, at thirteen-and-a-half. She is in sixth grade and will graduate from primary school this summer. Like her sister, she refuses to commit to secondary school. Her teacher and her parents hope they can change her mind as the time draws closer, but her siblings know how stubborn she can be and doubt that she will do so. What Vanessa does look forward to are the afternoons she spends with her nephew. Ever since he was born in March 2010, she has been his primary caregiver. At the time, Rosa and Modesto were living with his parents, and Vanessa woke up early each morning to pick Cristian up from their house and bring him back to her parents' home. She would feed him and get him dressed before school started. Doña Goma cared for him until classes ended at noon. Vanessa would come running home and go directly to him. Now, at nearly two years old, he calls Vanessa "mama" and calls Rosa by her name. Whenever Cristian comes up in conversation, most of the women around town comment on how Vanessa instinctually knew how to care for him. They speculate that she is touched with the gift of being a midwife. Doña Goma's sister, doña Flora, is the last local midwife residents use. Most women go to the hospital now to give birth, even though it is very expensive. Ever since Rosa first became pregnant and her aunt began caring for her, Vanessa has shown an intense interest in midwifery. Many residents are pleased to see this, because she is the first young woman in the town to show any interest in learning the trade. Flora is sixty-five and believes that in two or three years she will be too old to continue delivering babies. Between caring for Cristian, school, and helping doña Goma with housework and weaving, it is hard for Vanessa to imagine time for anything else. For now, Vanessa's response is *"quien sabe"* (who knows).

As always, the boys drift in and out of the kitchen. When everyone is done eating, only Lucas, Goma, Modesto, and I remain. They are teaching me more about the *xok k'in* and explaining how these predictions can alter their planting schedule. Last year they had the first good harvest in four years, and they are hopeful that this one will be the same. Doña Goma, meanwhile, puts up the leftovers and heads to the bathhouse. Tonight, as on all other nights, she is the last one to bathe. She likes to wait until after she finishes cooking because it gets so hot next to the fire. On this night, she will wash the dishes instead of leaving them for the morning. She is expecting a tour at 8:30 a.m. and wants to be prepared. The tours have become second nature to doña Goma and the family, and she has been teaching gringos to make tortillas for more than eight years now. She enjoys joking with them about how many tortillas she needs daily and how long it would take if she had to rely on their help. I sat in on the tour a few days before and noticed that she smiled for the camera and directed the tourists to take advantage of various photo opportunities before she moved on to the next part of the process. I ask her about this as we finish the dishes, and she says that the photos no longer bother her. She marvels, "How many places in the world has my face been? I never would have thought that people from all these other countries would know who I am."

With that, she laughs and dries her hands on her nightshirt. *"Tak a wenel, xunan* (you should sleep, *xuna*); you have to go to the milpa with Lucas tomorrow, right?" I agree and remind her that she has a big day tomorrow as well. First, a group of seven will arrive at 8:30 a.m. for the tour, and then she has to go to Temozón to visit doña Flora. The next stop is Valladolid to make a payment on a loan and then home to make lunch. In the afternoon there is a meeting with agents from Secretaria de Desarrolla Social (Social Development Secretariat, SEDESOL) checking up on the garden project. Finally, in the evening she is hosting a volunteer who is here working on the nature trail project. When I finish this long list, she jokes that everyone comes to Ek'Balam to work on a different project, but managing the requirements that come along with each group seems to be her project.

Most everyone has settled into his or her hammock to watch television. Half of us are in the blockhouse and the other half are in the thatch house. Both houses have televisions, but the blockhouse now has satellite cable. Everyone has been enjoying this for the past three months. Eugenio pays for it because he says his younger brothers, sisters, niece, and nephew can learn from it. The Discovery Channel was ushered in 2012 by airing and re-airing a series called *2012: The Maya Prophecies*. We are enjoying the episode about crystal skulls tonight, and the others are filling me in on some of the episodes I have yet to see. Modesto rolls over in his hammock and asks "what do you think, Cuma? Will the world end in December like they say? Do you believe it?"

I reply *"min crextik* (I don't believe it). But plenty of people are wondering about it." To that Eugenio exclaims, "Maybe they will all come here to find out. That would be a lot of tourists." The advertisement is over and the show starts again. We return our attention to it and fall asleep thinking of crystal skulls, the apocalypse, and hammock sales.

THE DEVELOPMENT OF AN ENTREPRENEURIAL SPIRIT

The eight years from 2004 to 2012 in Ek'Balam have seen a slow but steady shift toward reliance on tourism for economic benefit that is in some cases replacing subsistence farming and other pre-tourism earning strategies. In other cases, it is allowing for additional spending on items that were previously out of reach financially, such as household appliances and tuition fees for study beyond sixth grade. The main avenue for economic participation in tourism is the creation and sale of hammocks and other handicrafts. The second option for participation is through the community-based tourism project. Many alternative tourism initiatives like this CBT project can also be classified as pro-poor tourism (Ashley, Boyd, and Goodwin 2000; Ashley and Maxwell 2001). This concept emerged as a critical response to previous literature that characterized tourism development in the "developing world" as negative. A main idea from pro-poor tourism is that "businesses at all levels and scales of operation have the potential to contribute to poverty alleviation" (Scheyvens and Russell 2012, 418). In the case of indigenous tourism, the concurrent goals of sustainable economic development and valuation of cultural and natural heritage can work together to alleviate poverty (Ceballos-Lascurain 1996).

The development of mass tourism in Quintana Roo has created numerous opportunities for migration, and most (if not all) communities in the region have migratory populations (Castellanos 2010a). The cycle of out-migration from rural pueblos to Cancún for employment in the tourist industry has immense effects not only on those navigating a new urban life but also on the families they leave behind. Alicia Re Cruz (1996, 114) states that the "reconfiguration of the family among those who migrate breaks the bonds of the original village family." Shifting gender dynamics within the household are apparent in the wake of economic change, which is one of the reasons assessing development outcomes at the household level can provide a more complete analysis.

In the 1980s, ethnographers converged on the household as a unit of study. Since then, there has been a spectrum of studies of the relationship between the household and the outside world. Inherent in these studies is debate over the inside-outside dichotomy. On one hand, Tracy Bachrach Ehlers (2000) presents the household as insular and closed and as having a high level of separation from the outside world. At the other end of the spectrum is Walter E. Little's research in Aguas Calientes, Guatemala. There, he found the household to be open and public, even presenting an influential argument for the household as a stage for performing tourism (Little 2000). June C. Nash's research occupies the middle ground between these two (Nash 2001; Nash and Fernandez-Kelly 1983). The household is usefully understood as a productive unit, although this, too, has varied in the literature. Alice Littlefield's study of the hammock industry in Yucatán (Littlefield 1978) positioned the household as an engine of economic production, while Richard R. Wilk (1997) presents the household as the center of ecological production. In both cases, the household is a tool that facilitates analysis of the roles of women.

Both of these views perpetuate the gender-streaming approach commonly found in development initiatives, which count on women to be both productive and reproductive engines. This perspective is similarly expressed in the literature as the "triple burden" of women throughout Latin America (Bose and Acosta-Belén 1995; Hays-Mitchell 2002). The manifestation of these trends in Ek'Balam is visible in the diversification of household production and income (Schüren 2003). The economic crises during Latin America's "Lost Decade" of the 1980s led to a shifting role for women as wage laborers. In the town of San Cosme, Mexico, Frances Rothstein (2007) recorded a doubling of women's share of labor, from 12 percent in 1980 to 25 percent in 1989. She also reported that half of the town's young women are in the labor force. While neo-liberal reforms in Mexico and elsewhere increase the availability of work for women in the non-agrarian labor force, many are "confined to low-paying jobs, without protection, security, or hope of mobility" (Safa 2002, 141).

Within the agrarian sector, the opportunities for formal-sector employment are even worse (Stephen 1993). Similar to Rothstein's experience in San Cosme, the roles within the new household earning strategies are dictated not only by internal family dynamics but also by external forces, the most predominant of which is tourism. What is unique about this case is the fact that only between three and five women in the village hold jobs in the formal economy at any given time, employed in the two foreign-owned hotels in Ek'Balam. The rest are participating in the local, informal economy, as is common in similar communities throughout Latin America (Biles 2009). The most common means for participation is the production and sale of hammocks, which has become a main source of income for many families. The opportunity to sell hammocks directly to tourists—rather than through intermediaries who previously pocketed most of the profits—has created a new entrepreneurial spirit in the village. The new income generated through handicraft sales—women's work—has also been the primary source of capital formation for individuals who want to start small businesses. Six households now have goods for sale out of their homes, whereas in 2004 there were only two. They range from an operation that sells a few bottles of Coke and snacks to stores that contract with the grocery store in Temozón to sell all manner of groceries on consignment.

After a few years of receiving a small payment for the village tour (about US$2 per tour) and regular tips in varying amounts from the visitors, doña Gomercinda was ready to make the purchase she had been anxiously awaiting: a refrigerator. This expenditure of US$300 bought on credit from an appliance store in Valladolid was a very big decision for the family, but don Lucas agreed that it was up to doña Gomercinda to determine how to spend these earnings:

> Well, she works hard to take care of the house and our family but is always happy to stop what she is doing and welcome the gringos who come to see how we live and how she makes tortillas. Whew, for years she has said, "when can we find the money to buy my refrigerator?" And now, thanks to the gringos, we have one. She is so happy now when she goes in to get Coke from the fridge to sell to someone. And with the money she makes from selling snacks to the kids, well that helps with the money we pay [for the refrigerator] every 15 days. It truly is Doña Gomercinda's fridge. ~Don Lucas [Transcriptions 2009-0704 (9:08)]

Within weeks of purchasing the refrigerator, doña Gomercinda was buying Coke and juices to sell to neighbors. Other households are following this trend, and women are mainly involved in the purchase and resale of goods. Indeed, women's participation in the formal and informal tourism economy generated the majority of the material capital used to start these micro-enterprises.

These changes can be seen in figure 7.1, which shows the three most important sources of income in Ek'Balam and the change between 2004 and 2012. "Milpa," which has declined slightly but steadily, refers to individuals whose main household earning strategy is the production of maize. The category "Commerce" is used to represent individuals who have income from some form of commerce in which they are directly involved. "Crafts" refers to anyone who produces and sells handicrafts to tourists. The number of households engaged in this strategy

Change in income categories

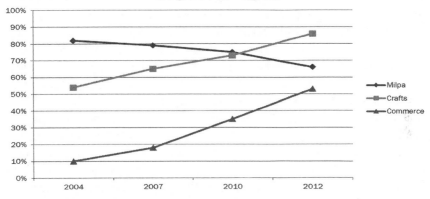

FIGURE 7.1. *Change in income categories, 2004–2012*

is higher than the number of those engaged in commerce. Examples of crafts for sale are hammocks, purses, and embroidered dresses, or *huipiles*. The households engaged in commerce sell soda, packaged snacks, or other consumable goods. One important difference is that almost all sales in the Crafts category are to visitors, while nearly all sales in the Commerce category are to residents. The percentages shown in figure 7.1 represent those of the collaborator sample (n = 100) that reported income from one or more of these categories. As discussed earlier, most households engage in multiple economic activities.

The ever-increasing stream of tourists arriving in Ek'Balam and other previously remote villages to purchase handicrafts is not only increasing the availability of cash but is leading to familial changes, such as the redistribution of wealth and a shift in traditional gender roles. In this sense, Ek'Balam is becoming more like high-volume tourist destinations such as Guatemala, where Little (2000, 174) reports that household gender relations have shifted to such an extent that it is "possible for women to support children without the aid of men, making them more economically independent and powerful within the community." The ability of women to contribute financially to the household has resulted in additional educational opportunities for their children. There is a free public school in the village that children attend through the sixth grade. At that point it becomes rather costly to continue their studies because it means either securing daily transportation from Ek'Balam to a neighboring town where there is a school or staying with a family member who lives in that town. The increased income from handicrafts and other informal endeavors allows women to put money aside to handle these costs. In 2004 I knew of only two young people in the village who were in the process of completing their studies through the twelfth grade. In 2007 that number had jumped to five, and in 2009 I knew of nine students attending *"la prepa."*

The new economy that has emerged in the wake of agrarian reform and the concurrent development of tourism is similar to what Sol Tax (1972, ix) identified as a system of "penny capitalism"; that is, "a society which is 'capitalist' on a microscopic scale." Other scholars working in predominantly Maya communities throughout Yucatán have noted similar economic shifts. Ellen R. Kintz (1998, 598), writing about her work in Cobá, Yucatán, also calls on Tax's term when discussing the increase in economic enterprises initiated by women (Kintz 1998, 598). She states that while historically women were excluded from the cash economy, they "have now become the managers of cash which flows into their household from a variety of sources" (Kintz 1998, 597). Various factors contribute to the new role of women as "managers" of the household economy, not the least of which is migration (Gaskins 2003). Although the frequency of migration in Ek'Balam is lower than in other nearby *ejidos*, there are a number of households headed by women the majority of the time.

The house at the entrance to the village is that of the Tuz May family. There is a small *palapa* hung with multicolored hammocks, which is the first thing a visitor sees of the pueblo. Houses of either block or thatch line up along the north, east, and south sides of the plaza, while the west side is dominated by the house of doña Carolina. Her looming butter-colored edifice stands in stark contrast to the whitewashed poles of don Wiliam's thatch house with political propaganda painted on the front. Eight of the houses around the plaza have hammocks displayed under small thatch-roof *palapas* in hopes of making a sale to the occasional passer-by. The positioning of houses took place long before the first tourist arrived in Ek'Balam, and the advantageous placement of some houses for selling hammocks is both a product of luck and a point of contention for some of the women whose houses are in other parts of the pueblo that do not get as much tourist traffic. Competition is fierce when it comes to selling hammocks, and women who bring hammocks from areas off the plaza are not welcome by others who have deemed a group of tourists as "theirs." This is a difficult situation for the tourists as well. When the occasional group comes into town and stops in the plaza—the only obvious place to pull over—they are all but attacked, and one does not have to speak Maya to understand that insults and harsh words are being exchanged between the women who were first on the scene and those who came later.

The production and sale of hammocks is a main source of income for many families in the village. Some women rely on hammocks for all their staples, such as corn and sugar. Doña Filomena's husband leaves the village for work and returns *cada quincera*, or every fifteen days. Although his earnings for work on a ranch are good, he is not working a milpa, so the family must purchase their corn locally from other families or in the neighboring city of Temozón. Doña Filomena talked to me in 2007 about the economic importance of her weaving:

"If you make two hammocks, one will buy a bag of corn, which right now goes for about 170 pesos [US$17]. Then from the other I take all of my expenses—sugar, coffee, bread, everything. It is only when I sell a hammock for 350 pesos [US$35] that I can get the money to buy more tubes [of thread] to start another hammock" ~Doña Filomena [Transcriptions 2007-0629 (12:00)].

The opportunity to sell hammocks to tourists has created a new entrepreneurial spirit in the village. As recently as 2004, hammocks and the traditional embroidered *huipil* were the only crafts produced, but now the artisans of Ek'Balam extend their talent to the creation of mini-fruit hammocks, crocheted purses, soda tab belts, and embroidered tank tops for sale to visiting gringos.

SOCIAL CAPITAL AND THE TRIPLE BOTTOM LINE

Although indigenous tourism and CBT development are posited as an alternative to previous models, the rate of participation and improved outcomes are sometimes questionable. Sustainability is the key factor that distinguishes these projects, but it is not necessarily a guaranteed outcome of this approach (Jones 2005). Many projects use the TBL to measure outcomes and a project's potential for long-term sustainability. The TBL was first coined in the context of corporate responsibility for sustainability (Elkington 1999), but it was quickly adopted as a metric to gauge community quality-of-life outcomes of tourism initiatives (Tyrrell, Paris, and Biaett 2012). The TBL is based on the "Pillars of Sustainability" from the World Commission on Environment and Development's (WCED) 1987 report "Our Common Future," which is often referred to as the Bruntland Report (Hall 1999). Sustainable development is defined in this publication as development that "meets the needs of the present without compromising the ability of future generations to meet their own needs" (Bruntland 1987, 43) and includes environmental quality, economic prosperity, and social well-being (Rogers and Ryan 2001). Unfortunately, a monetary unit of measure is generally prioritized, even though the literature suggests that social outcomes are not quantifiable because of their variation across a community (Vanclay 2004). Further, the identification of appropriate indicators of social outcomes is an obstacle to functional TBL metrics (Dwyer 2005). A final obstacle to a realistic assessment of TBL metrics is a positive or optimistic bias in reporting outcomes (Faux 2005). Some scholars are moving toward a quadruple bottom line (QBL) metric that incorporates the role of culture in determining a project's ultimate sustainability (Engelbrecht 2011; Scrimgeour and Iremonger 2004; Teriman, Yigitcanlar, and Mayere 2009). The inclusion of cultural considerations makes the QBL model ideal for assessing indigenous tourism initiatives by acknowledging the relationship between social and cultural capital.

This important nuance in the relationship between project design and the community in which a project is implemented can be usefully understood in terms of bridging versus bonding social capital. Bonding social capital refers to the creation of links between groups within a larger homogeneous group (Beugelsdijk and Smulders 2003). Bridging social capital creates links between heterogeneous groups (Coffé and Geys 2007; Grootaert and Van Bastelaer 2002). The ultimate goal of improving social capital vis-à-vis a community-based development initiative generally assumes that both bridging and bonding forms of social capital will be strengthened (Jones 2005). These were dual outcome goals for the sustainability of the CBT project in Ek'Balam. Discussion of the values, role, and complexities of social capital in sustainable tourism development is increasingly recognized as important (see McGehee, Knollenberg, and Komorowski 2015; Ooi, Laing, and Mair 2015)

Sustainable development is "the process of utilizing the social, economic, and environmental resources in a country or region to be able to continue to meet the needs of its residents over time" (Bojanic 2011, 989). The ultimate goal of development is always important. More often than not, the stated goals of the funding agency or organization bear little resemblance to the implicit benefits envisioned by community leaders and liaisons.

In 2001 the Mexican Secretary of Tourism (SECTUR) initiated the Pueblos Mágicos (Magic Villages) program in conjunction with state and local governments. SECTUR (2012) defined these villages as places "with symbolism, legends, history, important events, day-to-day life—in other words, 'magic' in its social and cultural manifestations, with great opportunities for tourism." The goal of this program is to revalue and recapture the culture and tradition of these villages that have "always been in the collective imagination of the nation as a whole and represent fresh and different alternatives for local and foreign visitors. More than simply cultural revival is a tribute to those who live in these beautiful places throughout Mexico and have guarded for all of us the rich culture and history they contain" (SECTUR 2012).

Izamal was inaugurated as the tenth Pueblo Mágico in 2002, and currently there are fifty Pueblos Mágicos throughout Mexico. In 2010 the new municipal commissioner in Ek'Balam, don Alonzo, began talking with me about this program. He is a guide at the archaeological zone who went to Izamal for training. He came back excited about the prospect of Ek'Balam becoming a Pueblo Mágico. Authorities consider five criteria when a village applies to the program: traditional architecture, emblematic buildings, festivals and traditions, production of artisan crafts, and maintenance of culinary traditions. Part of the catalyst for the new urban plan was the idea that if Ek'Balam met these criteria, it would be on the way to gaining this designation.

The most interesting aspect of this process is the diachronic nature of the plans for authenticity. In thinking about the space that would be included as part of the Pueblo Mágico ideal, the urban area is included along with the rest of the *ejido*

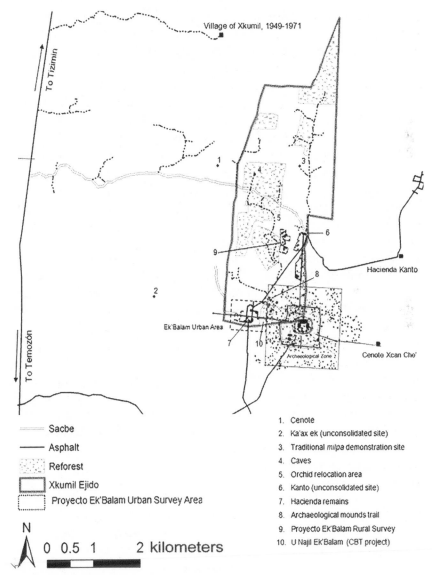

.... Sacbe

———— Asphalt

Reforest

Xkumil Ejido

Proyecto Ek'Balam Urban Survey Area

N

0 0.5 1   2 kilometers

1. Cenote
2. Ka'ax ek (unconsolidated site)
3. Traditional *milpa* demonstration site
4. Caves
5. Orchid relocation area
6. Kanto (unconsolidated site)
7. Hacienda remains
8. Archaeological mounds trail
9. Proyecto Ek'Balam Rural Survey
10. U Najil Ek'Balam (CBT project)

FIGURE 7.2. *Ek'Balam's ecosystem of authenticity*

and the archaeological zone. Figure 7.2 is a map of the key places that are part of this plan. In the south are the urban area of Ek'Balam and the monuments in the ceremonial center of the archaeological zone. Included here as points on the map are the CBT project, the well and hacienda foundation in the center of town, and the ball court. In the north is the rest of the *ejido* and Hacienda Kanto. In the farthest north portion is the abandoned village site of X'Kumil. Key points in this region are caves, *cenotes,* milpas, unconsolidated monuments, and reforestation areas. All told, the map contains features that span time periods from the Terminal Classic period (circa A D 1000), the early Hispanic period (circa 1600), the hacienda era (circa 1850), post-Revolutionary land reform (circa 1930), to the present. Residents, however, are ambivalent about assigning periods to the map. They feel that without these designations the map creates a picture of the entirety of Ek'Balam's heritage. This map is an image of the ecosystem of authenticity.

In the minds of many Ek'Balam residents, the ability to maintain this authenticity is dependent on their use of cultural capital and creation of symbolic capital. As *dueños* (caretakers) of this ecosystem, they are acting as stewards of all facets of their environment: cultural, ecological, and economic. They are fulfilling their role as "heirs of heritage," and, most important, they are Maya-enough.

DEFINING SUCCESS

Each of the numerous stakeholders in the development process has a different idea of what the outcomes should be. Financial benefit is, of course, important; however, overgeneralizations are made about community pride, valuation of indigenous heritage, increased connections to the past, and educational opportunities. Most projects that hope to serve as vehicles to successful development, however we define it, fall into one of two categories: external and internal. The category of external projects (into which most initiatives fall) is defined as those projects whose design and plan for implementation is generated by an external group. Internal projects are those designed and implemented locally. This is not to say that all resources come from within the village, only that residents determined the focus of the project. Proponents of the community-based and participatory approaches to development argue that the internal nature of a project gives it a greater chance of success because of its consideration of local needs. In Ek'Balam, however, this is not the case. Both types of projects enjoy nearly the same level of success. Duncan MacLean Earle offers an alternative to these two approaches to community development. He argues that the relations a community has with external actors—such as development agency staff—are key to improving conditions in a community (Earle 1984).

The ultimate goal of development is always important. More often than not, the stated goals of the funding agency or organization bear little resemblance to the implicit benefits envisioned by community leaders and liaisons. Earle and Jean M. Simonelli provide illustrations of this difference in their discussion of the interactions between Zapatista community groups and regional NGOs. According to them, "Social transformation without economic outcome was useless. Economic outcome with culturally inappropriate social transformation was also unacceptable. But in spite of the contradictions, group after group chose to eat from [the NGOs'] fast-food menu of projects" (Earle and Simonelli 2005, 142).

When tourism is positioned as the vehicle to development, this vision is all the more crucial. It is undesirable to develop a rural Maya village to the point that it no longer feels rural to the visitor because of the frequent association of rurality with indigeneity (Earle 1984; Faust 1998). What looks like success in a different context could actually mean disaster for tourism development. In these cases, the entire community is the destination. This includes the actual CBT project but also the houses a visitor must pass on the way to the project. By extension, the people living in those houses must also maintain a certain image in order to fit in. Both the physical and social realms of the village must together form this ecosystem of authenticity.

By understanding the successes and failures of this case, we can potentially influence how future projects are designed and measured. It is important to include cases like this one because it is exemplary of indigenous tourism in both the design and the attraction (Taylor 2017). In the case of Ek'Balam, the regional importance of archaeological and indigenous (or cultural) tourism is creating a demand for services in this community and, in many cases, revaluing indigenous culture. At the same time, the development of indigenous tourism (through the CBT project) is exacerbating existing social tensions and decreasing social cohesion. While this project has not achieved the success locals and agency staff had hoped for, it did not fail on all counts. If we assess this project based on the TBL, we find some interesting results. The first goal of the project was to stem out-migration among young men in the community. The associates of the CBT project identified this goal themselves in response to the rising rates of young people leaving the village to work on the coast in the tourism industry. This goal has been achieved, and each year more young people are able to find work locally.

The ever-increasing stream of tourists arriving in Ek'Balam and other pre-viously remote villages to purchase handicrafts is not only increasing the availability of cash but is leading to the redistribution of wealth and a shift in traditional gender roles.

This project has been a success and a failure in terms of both economic and social metrics. It has not yielded the widespread economic benefit to the com-munity envisaged by the funding agency. It has arguably paved the way for other sources of income that are accessible to a larger portion of the commu-nity. To assess the outcomes of this project, we must contextualize them within the broader cultural reality of the community, similar to the ways we must understand indigenous communities generally. These are diverse collections of families and households constructing meaningful lives with the resources at hand rather than examples of idealized indigeneity.

Cultural characteristics, language, traditional dress, and an agrarian lifestyle define indigeneity throughout Mesoamerica. Sheldon Annis (1987, 73) calls the milpa "the productive engine of colonial Indianness." This may be the case in

Guatemala; however, in Mexico the *ejido* is the "productive engine" of Indian-ness. In Amatlan, Mexico, Alan R. Sandstrom (1991, 202) found that people organize village life around non-capitalist principles and accordingly "allocate their scarce resources toward alternative ends according to rational principles." Among these rational principles is the knowledge that while increased agricultural output is the logical means for increasing wealth, this does not persuade individuals to stop planting corn in place of more productive crops. Decision-making, according to Sandstrom (1991), is based on "milpa logic" instead of market logic. Because of this, villagers must generate cash income and are dependent on political and economic forces from the nation's power centers. Through the maintenance of a specific lifestyle among indigenous groups based on economic need and the necessary tie to government-administered lands, the state functions as an agent of power that provides the context for "everyday struggle" (Joseph and Nugent 1994).

If we see land reform and Mexico's *ejido* as purveyors of popular culture—that is, the culture of the populous—then we see how the state is further implicated in the creation of identity in rural regions in the wake of numerous changes to the land system. More recently, a variety of external actors have worked to commoditize this indigenous identity for the promotion of tourism. If success in this context is determined by economic income, then these small, indigenous tourism projects will rarely be able to compete with the region's massive tourism industry. If we define success based only on social or cultural outcomes, then we will certainly see that there are changes in the community that some would say are shifting cultural traditions. Rural studies of popular culture often frame this as folklore, or what Néstor García Canclini and others call "apocalyptic" views of mass culture as a destroyer of the authentic; however, it seems that capitalism has not succeeded in eradicating tradition (García Canclini 1993; Overmyer-Velázquez 2011).

Being Maya, Getting By

The Yucatec Maya in the states of Campeche, Yucatán, and Quintana Roo have long had the attention of anthropologists. Since 1970, they have also caught the attention of tourists, as the Maya Riviera was developed into a world-class destination. Now, in the Mexico of multiculturalism and neoliberal governance, indigenous groups have become the focus of the state in a new way (Gledhill 2004; Mattiace and Salazar 2015). The creation of local or grassroots support through an emphasis on community-based development initiatives affords the state an image of being hands-off. The maintenance of this focus, however, is dependent on residents' actions as proper citizens and, as Quetzil E. Castañeda and Jennifer P. Mathews (2013) termed them, as "heirs of heritage." Implicit in the mandate to participate in development is an agreement to maintain a level of community cohesion and indigeneity that ultimately limits their agency over the process of development (Overmyer-Velázquez 2007). This indigeneity is itself tied up in tourist expectations, which in turn guide the decrees of external institutions. The mandate is above all to be Maya.

DOI: 10.5876/9781607327721.c008

Perhaps, as with indigeneity, the concept of community is both strategic essentialism and essential strategy (Fischer 1999; Castañeda 2007). For the federally funded development agency, the use of "community" results in a cultural and racially bounded entity that can be targeted for development. The unwieldy aspects are avoided because the agency is not responsible for designating exactly which residents will be included in the development process; instead, that decision will be left to the community. For the individuals and households involved, claiming membership in the community and, even further, calling the community a Pueblo Maya is an essential strategy. By claiming this identity, individuals are able to use their indigeneity to attract support in the form of funding for their community-based tourism (CBT) project, labor from volunteer tourists interested in community development, and assistance from tourists hoping to partake in a different, authentic, and sustainable form of tourism.

Since 1994, when the Instituto Nacional de Anthropología e Historia (INAH) opened the archaeological zone to the public, residents of Ek'Balam have faced a variety of changes in household economics. Since the CBT project opened ten years later, there has been a shift toward reliance on tourism for economic benefit. Some families maintain a traditional lifestyle and still rely on their own crops each year. These *ejidatarios* take the few odd jobs they can find to earn cash they need to supplement their crops and purchase clothes, shoes, and other necessities. Other households have transitioned completely to a reliance on the tourism economy. These individuals no longer farm any land and instead dedicate their time to work at the CBT project. This process leaves households that have made the switch to tourism with few alternative economic strategies in the face of a volatile tourism market.

Events in 2008 and 2009, starting with the economic downturn and followed quickly by the H1N1 Influenza outbreak, left the region in dire economic straits because of the sharp decline in tourism. According to the UN World Tourism Organization's World Tourism Barometer, international tourism arrivals declined worldwide by 8 percent between January and April 2009 (UN World Tourism Organization 2009, 3). Because of the decline in the value of the peso, US dollar spending declined by 7.6 percent in Mexico, representing a forecasted 9 percent decline in tourism receipts in the country's gross national product (GNP) by the end of 2009 (UN World Tourism Organization 2009). During the summer of 2009, I found families that were literally going hungry because they had not sold a single hammock in more than two months. For households that no longer produced food on their own land and whose migratory husbands and sons lacked work on the coast, alternative earning strategies were few. This questions the validity of the argument for tourism as a sustainable tool for development.

Power is one of the most noteworthy inhibitors of sustainability; tourism development decision-making is inherently political. The literature has yet to grasp the "place-specific interactions of power and politics and how these aspects shape and define the outcomes of the process" (Ruhanen 2013, 91). Tourism is increasingly viewed by local governments as a requirement for local economic development (Palomino Villavicencio and López Pardo 2012; Reid 2003). Underlying this requirement is a misconception that governance can go beyond commercial interest, but governments have generally not been successful at "giving equal attention to the triple bottom line, instead tending overtly to focus on the economic aspects" (Ruhanen 2013, 90). The variations in opinions about the project and its real and perceived benefits make it difficult to assess the actual sustainability of community-based tourism in this village. A useful consideration is an examination of the differences between direct and indirect benefits from the tourism project.

FINAL THOUGHTS AND FURTHER RESEARCH

At an earlier stage in this research, I concluded that an anthropological approach to understanding the complex negotiations with tourism in everyday life could ease what would otherwise be a rough transition along the "folk-urban continuum" into the hyper-real world of virtual tradition fostered by global tourism (Taylor 2008, 113); however, I am not sure that I can draw the same conclusion at this point in my research. Because of the agency involved in this process and the fact that an individual can seemingly move in and out of authenticity as needed, the idea of individuals solely being "folk," "urban," or somewhere in between does not make sense. Instead of being a fixed spectrum on which tourists, archaeologists, ethnographers, and others place and re-place Mayas depending on their progress toward modernity, perhaps the folk-urban continuum itself is the fluid component.

Ethnographers in Mesoamerica are famously concerned with duality, with the folk-urban dichotomy but one example. We are preoccupied with authentic and inauthentic renditions of culture, with tradition and modernity, with Maya-ness as essential or constructed. In the context of tourism studies, the front stage/backstage contrast is incorporated into the dichotomous nature of our work as well. Many scholars write about their subjects as fixed. García Canclini (1990), Redfield (1950), and others discuss the movements of people on a scale in and out of modernity. While these authors recognize the agency in the process, they still frame "traditional" and "modern" as discreet locations on a continuum that, because of the spatiality of the conceptual framework, cannot be dually occupied (Little 2004b, 264). What Walter E. Little (2004b, 87, original emphasis) points out, however, is that "in Antigua the normal routine of local people *is* tourism," a fact that changes the distinctions between home and work. In contrast to Edward M. Bruner's (1996, 2005) conception of a tourism border zone as an "empty stage waiting for performance," Little (2004b, 265) sees the traditionally dichotomous spheres of tourism and tradition, or front stage and backstage, as mixed up and, really, "just the way life is." I, too, argue for this *mezcla*, or mix-up, when examining tourism in the public and domestic spheres of everyday life.

The fluidity of a continuum recognized to be a sliding scale of sorts elicits a different identity—as in identifier—depending on both the placement and the agent doing the placing. When a Yucatec Maya man is in charge of organizing a traditional Maya rain ceremony, in the action of reaching down and replacing his rubber flip-flops with rope sandals he is sliding the continuum beneath his feet and setting it to "folk." Later, when he is asked to coordinate a group retreat for CDI's project staff, he picks up his day planner and cell phone and turns the continuum up to "urban." If these are the types of identity-identifiers we are using, are we not saying that his identity is based on ability, knowledge, and financial resources? If this is the case, I worry that we are slipping down the slope toward an image of the uneducated Indio as the inhabitants of folk communities.

For all the cautionary tales of sustainable development turned unsustainable and participation gone awry, few questions are asked about the foundation of this and other indigenous tourism development projects. Money is the foundation of the community-based tourism project in Ek'Balam and similar projects; the money is based on tourists' spending. No one asked the question that was on everyone's mind: what if we build it and they do not come? The further implications of this scenario are dire. What if a family sells its land and shifts to complete reliance on the sale of hammocks? What if a farmer chooses to dedicate his parcel to conservation through a federal program that exchanges sapling trees for the promise not to cut them? He hopes that the biodiversity he is creating and conserving will be an attraction, but what if there is no one to attract? These terrible questions became part of the collective discourse in 2009 when the region was devastated by the Swine Flu (H1N1 Influenza) outbreak. Families enveloped by the tourism development machine suddenly had nothing to fall back on. Households that had been doing quite well selling handicrafts and groceries found themselves struggling to provide enough food for everyone in the household. For generations, households in this and other similar communities have prospered because of their diverse economic strategies. As tourism takes the place of traditional sources of income, some enjoy high times, but it would seem that everyone experiences the lean times. Is this what a sustainably developed community looks like? Is this successful indigenous tourism? And, to reply to the politician in attendance at the staged Ch'a Chaak ceremony in 2010, is *this* Maya? I fear that labeling the situation we found in 2009 as a success leads us to the slippery slope of mistaking poverty for indigeneity.

I have many interactions with tourists when I am in the field, and they invariably ask the same question when I explain what I am doing there: is tourism good for this village or bad? That is not a question I am capable of answering and certainly not something that will be the same for every household there. What I can say is that the events of 2009 and 2010 have left everyone talking about crisis. Would they have shared in the economic crisis felt everywhere if they were not engaged in tourism as a principal earning strategy? Probably. But they would still have had something to eat. On the other hand, none of the youth would be continuing their studies, learning other languages, or imagining any future other than being a farmer. The lingering state of crisis has led leaders in the community to examine what is happening there and to step up their actual engagement in the decision-making process. The word *apoyo* there seemed to mean a gift or grant of money a few years ago. Now people, especially young people, use it to refer to assistance, both monetary and through the donation of physical labor and knowledge. They took it upon themselves to decide how they would organize the Ch'a Chaak and how they would demonstrate their Maya-ness for the guests they welcomed.

I have argued in this book for a reevaluation of the way we think about Maya-ness and the way we position Mayas in the Maya World. To help us in this repositioning process, I relied on our guides, the Ay Mena family, to provide a vision of what daily life is like here at this intersection of tourism and development. We met Goma, who is fiercely independent, happy to host tourists, and yet still maintains the importance of many traditional aspects of life. We met Goma's sons, each of whom shows a different facet of life choices available to these young men. During the counting days in the first month of 2012, we learned from Lucas about what traditional farming means to him and how he foresees his sons continuing to farm their land. In the midst of this are discussions about 2012, crystal skulls, the mysterious Maya, and whether the grandchildren will learn Maya. Ultimately, we learned that rather than thinking about the impact of tourism on the community, we should instead focus on the ways residents are able to incorporate this phenomenon into their already full lives and livelihoods. We can bound "the community" of Ek'Balam based on its own terms instead of relying on definitions available externally. Ek'Balam is a village and an archaeological zone and an ex-hacienda and a community. Residents are never occupying only one of these aspects of their community at a given time.

What I have found in the context of my research on sustainable community development is that being Maya is an experience that is situational, context-specific, and above all driven by the meaning and power ascribed to the term by the person using it. Using this discussion as a starting point, this research provided insights into how the ideological conflicts surrounding economic development unfold in the negotiations between internal community politics and non-local social actors, which make that interface an essential object for inquiry. In addition, the conflicts implicit in conceptions of "community" as a target for development are made explicit through the systematic questioning of what exactly it means to be a member of a local, indigenous, or sustainable community in the process of being developed with the hope of being Maya and getting by.

References

Aas, Christina, Adele Ladkin, and John Fletcher. 2005. "Stakeholder Collaboration and Heritage Management." *Annals of Tourism Research* 32 (1): 28–48. https://doi.org/10 .1016/j.annals.2004.04.005.

Abel, Thomas, and John Richard Stepp. 2003. "A New Ecosystems Ecology for Anthropology." *Conservation Ecology* 7 (3): 12–25. https://doi.org/10.5751/ES-00579-070312.

Abraham, Anita, and Jean-Philippe Platteau. 2004. "Participatory Development: Where Culture Creeps." In *In Culture and Public Action*, ed. Vijayendra Rao and Michael Walton, 210–33. Stanford, CA: Stanford University Press.

Alexander, Rani T. 2006. "Maya Settlement Shifts and Agrarian Ecology in Yucatán, 1800–2000." *Journal of Anthropological Research* 62 (4): 449–70. https://doi.org/10.3998 /jar.0521004.0062.401.

Almazan, Marco A. 1997. "NAFTA and the Mesoamerican States System." *Annals of the American Academy of Political and Social Science* 550 (1): 42–50. https://doi.org/10.117 7/0002716297550001003.

Alonso Olvera, Alejandra. 2015. "Archaeological Conservation at Ek'Balam and Its Influence on the Perception of the Pre-Hispanic Past and Cultural Identity in the Maya

Communities of Hunukú, Ek'Balam, and Santa Rita." *Archeological Papers of the American Anthropological Association* 25 (1): 83–89. https://doi.org/10.1111/apaa.12050.

Anderson, Eugene N. 2005. *Political Ecology in a Yucatec Maya Community.* Tucson: University of Arizona Press.

Anderson, Mark. 2013. "Notes on Tourism, Ethnicity, and the Politics of Cultural Value in Honduras." In *Central America in the New Millennium: Living Transition and Reimagining Democracy,* ed. Jennifer L. Burrell and Ellen Moodie, 276–93. New York: Berghahn Books.

Annis, Sheldon. 1987. *God and Production in a Guatemalan Town,* 1st ed. Texas Pan American Series. Austin: University of Texas Press.

Aramberri, Julio. 2001. "The Host Should Get Lost: Paradigms in the Tourism Theory." *Annals of Tourism Research* 28 (3): 738–61. https://doi.org/10.1016/S0160-7383(00)00075-X.

Ardren, Traci. 2002. "Conversations about the Production of Archaeological Knowledge and Community Museums at Chunchucmil and Kochol, Yucatán, México." *World Archaeology* 34 (2): 379–400. https://doi.org/10.1080/0043824022000007161.

Armstrong-Fumero, Fernando. 2012. *Elusive Unity: Factionalism and the Limits of Identity Politics in Yucatán, Mexico.* Boulder: University Press of Colorado.

Arroyo, Lucinda, Oscar Fausto, Romano Segrado, and Ismael Chuc. 2013. "Unsustainable Littoral Tourism in Tulum, Mexico." *Papers de Turisme* 54: 88–108.

Asensio, José María, Cristóbal de Pedraza, and Diego de Landa. 1898. "Relaciones de Yucatán." Colección de Documentos Inéditos Relativos Al Descubrimiento, Conquista Y Organización de Las Antiguas Posesiones Españolas de Ultramar, 2nd Series. Madrid: La Real Academia de la Historia.

Ashley, Caroline, Charlotte Boyd, and Harold Goodwin. 2000. "Pro-Poor Tourism: Putting Poverty at the Heart of the Tourism Agenda." Natural Resource Perspectives. ODI Overseas Development Institute. Accessed June 21, 2018. https://www.odi.org/sites/odi.org.uk/files/odi-assets/publications-opinion-files/2861.pdf.

Ashley, Caroline, and Simon Maxwell. 2001. "Rethinking Rural Development." *Development Policy Review* 19 (4): 395–425. https://doi.org/10.1111/1467-7679.00141.

Babb, Florence. 2010. *The Tourism Encounter: Fashioning Latin American Nations and Histories.* Stanford, CA: Stanford University Press.

Baños Ramírez, Orthon. 1989. *Yucatán: Ejidos Sin Campesinos.* Agricultura Y El Estado. Merida, Yucatán, Mexico: Universidad Autónoma de Yucatán.

Baños Ramírez, Orthon. 1995. *Liberalismo, actores y política en Yucatán.* Tratados y memorias de investigacion, UCS. Merida, Yucatán, Mexico: Universidad Autónoma de Yucatán.

Baños Ramírez, Orthon. 1998. "PROCEDE: Gateway to Modernization of the Ejido? The Case of the Yucatán." In *The Future Role of the Ejido,* ed. Richard Snyder and Gabriel Torres, 31–48. San Diego: University of California Press.

Barrera Vázquez, Alfredo, ed. 1980. *Diccionario Maya Cordemexmaya-Español; Español-Maya.* Merida, Yucatán, Mexico: Ediciones Cordemex.

Barthel-Bouchier, Diane. 2016. *Cultural Heritage and the Challenge of Sustainability*. London: Routledge.

Baud, Jan M., and Johanna Louisa Ypeij, eds. 2009. *Cultural Tourism in Latin America: The Politics of Space and Imagery*. CEDLA Latin American Studies 96. Boston: Brill.

Belsky, Jill M. 1999. "Misrepresenting Communities: The Politics of Community-Based Rural Ecotourism in Gales Point Manatee, Belize." *Rural Sociology* 64 (4): 641–66. https://doi.org/10.1111/j.1549-0831.1999.tb00382.x.

Bennett, John W. 1966. "Further Remarks on Foster's 'Image of Limited Good.'" *American Anthropologist* 68 (1): 206–10. https://doi.org/10.1525/aa.1966.68.1.02a00290.

Berger, Dina. 2006. *The Development of Mexico's Tourism Industry: Pyramids by Day, Martinis by Night*. Basingstoke, UK: Palgrave Macmillan. https://doi.org/10.1057/9781403982865.

Berger, Dina, and Andrew Grant Wood. 2010. *Holiday in Mexico: Critical Reflections on Tourism and Tourist Encounters*. Durham, NC: Duke University Press.

Bernard, H. Russell. 2011. *Research Methods in Anthropology: Qualitative and Quantitative Approaches*. Lanham, MD: Altamira.

Beugelsdijk, Sjoerd, and Sjak Smulders. 2003. "Bridging and Bonding Social Capital: Which Type Is Good for Economic Growth." In *The Cultural Diversity of European Unity: Findings, Explanations, and Reflections from the European Values Study*, 6: 147–84. Vienna: Brill European Values Studies.

Bey, George J., Tara M. Bond, William M. Ringle, Craig A. Hanson, Charles W. Houck, and Carlos Peraza Lope. 1998. "The Ceramic Chronology of Ek Balam, Yucatan, Mexico." *Ancient Mesoamerica* 9 (1): 101–20. https://doi.org/10.1017/S0956536100001887.

Bey, George J., III, Craig A. Hanson, and William M. Ringle. 1997. "Classic to Postclassic at Ek Balam, Yucatan: Architectural and Ceramic Evidence for Defining the Transition." *Latin American Antiquity* 8 (3): 237–54. https://doi.org/10.2307/971654.

Biles, James J. 2009. "Informal Work in Latin America: Competing Perspectives and Recent Debates." *Geography Compass* 3 (1): 214–36. https://doi.org/10.1111/j.1749-8198.2008.00188.x.

Black, Stephen L. 1990. "The Carnegie Uaxactun Project and the Development of Maya Archaeology." *Ancient Mesoamerica* 1 (2): 257–76. https://doi.org/10.1017/S0956536100000298.

Bloom, Nicholas Dagen, ed. 2006. *Adventures into Mexico: American Tourism beyond the Border*. Lanham, MD: Rowman and Littlefield.

Bojanic, David. 2011. "Using a Tourism Importance–Performance Typology to Investigate Environmental Sustainability on a Global Level." *Journal of Sustainable Tourism* 19 (8): 989–1003. https://doi.org/10.1080/09669582.2011.584624.

Bonilla Jimenez, Carlos, Jose Luis Villa Aguijosa, and Jose Manuel Orozco Plascencia. 2010. "Impacto del programa de certificacion de derechos ejidales y titulacion de solares (PROCEDE) en los nucleos agrarios del municipio de Comala, Colima, México." In *Grupo Temático 18—Reforma agrária: territorialidades, identidades e desenvolvimiento sustentable*. Porto de Galinhas, PE, Brazil: Asociación Latinoamericana de Sociología Rural. Accessed June 21, 2018. http://docplayer.es/1931429-Grupo-tematico-18-reforma-agraria-territorialidades-identidades-e-desenvolvimiento-sustentable.html.

Bose, Christine E., and Edna Acosta-Belén. 1995. *Women in the Latin American Development Process*. Philadelphia: Temple University Press.

Bourdieu, Pierre L. 1986. "The Forms of Capital." In *Handbook of Theory and Research for the Sociology of Education*, ed. John G. Richardson, 241–58. New York: Greenwood.

Bramwell, Bill, and Bernard Lane. 2011. "Critical Research on the Governance of Tourism and Sustainability." *Journal of Sustainable Tourism* 19 (4–5): 411–21. https://doi.org/10.1080/09669582.2011.580586.

Breglia, Lisa. 2006. *Monumental Ambivalence: The Politics of Heritage*. Austin: University of Texas Press.

Breglia, Lisa. 2009. "Hacienda Hotels and Other Ironies of Luxury in Yucatán, México." In *Cultural Tourism in Latin America: The Politics of Space and Imagery*, ed. Jan M. Baud and Johanna Louisa Ypeij, 96: 245–62. CEDLA Latin American Studies. Boston: Brill. https://doi.org/10.1163/ej.9789004176409.i-324.83.

Brohman, John. 1996. "New Directions in Tourism for Third World Development." *Annals of Tourism Research* 23 (1): 48–70. https://doi.org/10.1016/0160-7383(95)00043-7.

Brown, Denise Fay. 1999. "Mayas and Tourists in the Maya World." *Human Organization* 58 (3): 295–304. https://doi.org/10.17730/humo.58.3.y21r5586l5941121.

Brown, Lorraine. 2013. "Tourism: A Catalyst for Existential Authenticity." *Annals of Tourism Research* 40: 176–90. https://doi.org/10.1016/j.annals.2012.08.004.

Brulotte, Ronda L. 2009. "'Yo Soy Nativo de Aquí': The Ambiguities of Race and Indigeneity in Oaxacan Craft Tourism." *Journal of Latin American and Caribbean Anthropology* 14 (2): 457–82. https://doi.org/10.1111/j.1935-4940.2009.01057.x.

Brulotte, Ronda L. 2012. *Between Art and Artifact: Archaeological Replicas and Cultural Production in Oaxaca, Mexico*. Austin: University of Texas Press.

Bruner, Edward M. 1996. "Tourism in Ghana." *American Anthropologist* 98 (2): 290–304. https://doi.org/10.1525/aa.1996.98.2.02a00060.

Bruner, Edward M. 2005. *Culture on Tour: Ethnographies of Travel*. Chicago: University of Chicago Press.

Brundtland, G. Harlem. 1987. *Our Common Future: The World Commission on Environment and Development*. Oxford: Oxford University Press.

Buckley, Ralf. 2012. "Sustainable Tourism: Research and Reality." *Annals of Tourism Research* 39 (2): 528–46. https://doi.org/10.1016/j.annals.2012.02.003.

Bueno, Christina. 2010. "Forjando Patrimonio: The Making of Archaeological Patrimony in Porfirian Mexico." *Hispanic American Historical Review* 90 (2): 215–45. https://doi.org/10.1215/00182168-2009-133.

Butler, Richard, and Thomas Hinch. 2007. *Tourism and Indigenous Peoples: Issues and Implications*. New York: Routledge.

Cabrera Valenzuela, Alejandro. 2013. "Ejidos y parentesco: Organización ejidal en X-Kumil, Yucatán (1935–1999)." Licentiate Report. Merida, Yucatán, Mexico: Universidad Autonoma de Yucatan.

Cancian, Frank. 1965. *Economics and Prestige in a Maya Community: The Religious Cargo System in Zinacantan*. Stanford, CA: Stanford University Press.

Cancian, Frank. 1972. *Change and Uncertainty in a Peasant Economy: The Maya Corn Farmers of Zinacantan*. Stanford, CA: Stanford University Press.

Cancian, Frank. 1992. *The Decline of Community in Zinacantán: Economy, Public Life, and Social Stratification, 1960–1987*. Stanford, CA: Stanford University Press.

Cant, Alanna. 2015. "One Image, Two Stories: Ethnographic and Touristic Photography and the Practice of Craft in Mexico." *Visual Anthropology* 28 (4): 277–85. https://doi.org/10.1080/08949468.2015.1052308.

Carr, Anna, Lisa Ruhanen, and Michelle Whitford. 2016. "Indigenous Peoples and Tourism: The Challenges and Opportunities for Sustainable Tourism." *Journal of Sustainable Tourism* 24 (8–9): 1067–79. https://doi.org/10.1080/09669582.2016.1206112.

Castañeda, Quetzil E. 1996. *In the Museum of Maya Culture: Touring Chichén Itzá*. Minneapolis: University of Minnesota Press.

Castañeda, Quetzil E. 2003. "New and Old Social Movements Measuring Pisté, from the 'Mouth of the Well' to the 107th Municipio of Yucatán." *Ethnohistory* 50 (4): 611–42. https://doi.org/10.1215/00141801-50-4-611.

Castañeda, Quetzil E. 2004. "'We Are Not Indigenous': An Introduction to the Maya Identity of Yucatan." *Journal of Latin American Anthropology* 9 (1): 36–63. https://doi.org/10.1525/jlca.2004.9.1.36.

Castañeda, Quetzil E. 2007. "Two Indians in the Age of Heritage: From Strategic Essentialism to Essential Strategy." Paper presented at the Heritage Tourism Conference, CEDLA, Amsterdam, June 14–16.

Castañeda, Quetzil E., and Jennifer Burtner. 2010. "Tourism as 'a Force for World Peace:' The Politics of Tourism, Tourism as Governmentality, and the Tourism Boycott of Guatemala." *Journal of Tourism and Peace Research* 1 (2): 1–21.

Castañeda, Quetzil E., and Jennifer P. Mathews. 2013. "Archaeology Meccas of Tourism: Exploration, Protection, and Exploitation." In *Tourism and Archaeology: Sustainable Meeting Grounds*, ed. Cameron Walker and Neil Carr, 37–64. Walnut Creek, CA: Left Coast.

Castellanos, M. Bianet. 2010a. *A Return to Servitude: Maya Migration and the Tourist Trade in Cancún*. Minneapolis: University of Minnesota Press.

Castellanos, M. Bianet. 2010b. "Don Teo's Expulsion: Property Regimes, Moral Economies, and Ejido Reform." *Journal of Latin American and Caribbean Anthropology* 15 (1): 144–69. https://doi.org/10.1111/j.1935-4940.2009.01056.x.

CDI (National Commission for the Development of Indigenous Villages). 2003. "U Najil Ek'Balam: Un centro turistico e indigena." In *Tourism and Archaeology: Sustainable Meeting Grounds*, ed. C. Walker and N. Carr, 37–64. Comisión Nacional para el

Desarrollo de los Pueblos Indígenas. Walnut Creek, CA: Left Coast Press. Accessed May 6, 2012. http://www.gob.mx/cdi/.

Ceballos-Lascurain, Hector. 1987. "The Future of Ecotourism." *Mexico Journal* 1 (17): 13–14.

Ceballos-Lascurain, Hector. 1996. "Tourism, Ecotourism, and Protected Areas: The State of Nature-Based Tourism around the World and Guidelines for Its Development." Paper presented at the Fourth World Congress on National Parks and Protected Areas, Caracas, Venezuela, February 10–21. https://doi.org/10.2305/IUCN .CH.1996.7.en.

Cernea, Michael. 1991. "Knowledge from Social Science for Development Policies and Projects." In *Putting People First: Sociological Variables in Rural Development*, 2nd ed., ed. Michael Cernea, 1–41. New York: Oxford University Press.

Chambers, Robert. 1994. "Participatory Rural Appraisal (PRA): Challenges, Potentials, and Paradigm." *World Development* 22 (10): 1437–54. https://doi.org/10.1016/0305-750 X(94)90030-2.

Cheong, So-Min, and Marc L. Miller. 2000. "Power and Tourism: A Foucauldian Observation." *Annals of Tourism Research* 27 (2): 371–90. https://doi.org/10.1016/S0160 -7383(99)00065-1.

Clancy, Michael J. 2001a. *Exporting Paradise: Tourism and Development in Mexico*. Oxford: Pergamon.

Clancy, Michael J. 2001b. "Mexican Tourism: Export Growth and Structural Change since 1970." *Latin American Research Review* 1 (36): 128–50.

Clark, Dylan J., and David S. Anderson. 2015. "Past Is Present: The Production and Consumption of Archaeological Legacies in Mexico." *Archeological Papers of the American Anthropological Association* 25 (1): 1–18. https://doi.org/10.1111/apaa.12042.

Clendinnen, Ina. 2003. *Ambivalent Conquests: Maya and Spaniard in Yucatan, 1517–1570*, vol. 61. Cambridge: Cambridge University Press. https://doi.org/10.1017/CBO97805 11800528.

Coffé, Hilde, and Benny Geys. 2007. "Toward an Empirical Characterization of Bridging and Bonding Social Capital." *Nonprofit and Voluntary Sector Quarterly* 36 (1): 121–39. https://doi.org/10.1177/0899764006293181.

Cohen, Eric. 1988. "Authenticity and Commoditization in Tourism." *Annals of Tourism Research* 15 (3): 371–86. https://doi.org/10.1016/0160-7383(88)90028-X.

Córdoba Azcárate, Matilde, Ana Garcia de Fuentes, and Juan Córdoba Ordóñez. 2014. "The Uneven Pragmatics of 'Affordable' Luxury Tourism in Inland Yucatán (México)." In *Elite Mobilities*, ed. Thomas Birtchnell and Javier Caletrío, 149–82. New York: Routledge.

Cornwall, Andrea. 2008. "Unpacking 'Participation': Models, Meanings, and Practices." *Community Development Journal: An International Forum* 43 (3): 269–83. https://doi.org /10.1093/cdj/bsn010.

Crang, Mike. 1997. "Picturing Practices: Research through the Tourist Gaze." *Progress in Human Geography* 21 (3): 359–73. https://doi.org/10.1191/030913297669603510.

Creamer, Winifred. 1987. "Mesoamerica as a Concept: An Archaeological View from Central America." *Latin American Research Review* 22 (1): 35–62.

Creed, Gerald W. 2006. *The Seductions of Community: Emancipations, Oppressions, Quandaries*. School of American Research Advanced Seminar Series. Santa Fe, NM: School of American Research Press.

Cromwell, Elizabeth, Patrick Kambewa, Richard Mwanza, and Rowland Chirwa. 2001. "Impact Assessment Using Participatory Approaches: 'Starter Pack' and Sustainable Agriculture in Malawi." AgREN Network Paper 112. London: Overseas Development Institute.

Das, Veena, and Deborah Poole. 2004. *Anthropology in the Margins of the State*. School of American Research Advanced Seminar Series. Santa Fe, NM: School of American Research Press.

De Certeau, Michel. 1984. *The Practice of Everyday Life*. Trans. Steven Rendall. Berkeley: University of California Press.

de la Peña, Guillermo. 1982. *A Legacy of Promises: Agriculture, Politics, and Ritual in the Morelos Highlands of Mexico*. Manchester: Manchester University Press.

Dinica, Valentina. 2009. "Governance for Sustainable Tourism: A Comparison of International and Dutch Visions." *Journal of Sustainable Tourism* 17 (5): 583–603. https://doi.org/10.1080/09669580902855836.

Dornbusch, Rudiger, and F. Leslie Helmers. 1991. *Open Economy: Tools for Policymakers in Developing Countries*. EDI Series in Economic Development. Washington, DC: World Bank.

Dwyer, Larry. 2005. "Relevance of Triple Bottom Line Reporting to Achievement of Sustainable Tourism: A Scoping Study." *Tourism Review International* 9 (1): 79–93. https://doi.org/10.3727/154427205774791726.

Earle, Duncan MacLean. 1984. "Cultural Logic and Ecology in Community Development: Failure and Success Cases among the Highland Maya." PhD dissertation, State University of New York at Albany.

Earle, Duncan MacLean, and Jean M. Simonelli. 2005. *Uprising of Hope: Sharing the Zapatista Journey to Alternative Development*. New York: Altamira.

Edensor, Tim. 2001. "Performing Tourism, Staging Tourism: (Re)producing Tourist Space and Practice." *Tourist Studies* 1 (1): 59–81. https://doi.org/10.1177/146879760100100104.

Ehlers, Tracy Bachrach. 2000. *Silent Looms: Women and Production in a Guatemalan Town*. Austin: University of Texas Press.

Elkington, John. 1999. *Cannibals with Forks: The Triple Bottom Line of Twenty First Century Business*. Mankato, MN: Capstone.

Engelbrecht, Marianne. 2011. "Towards the Quadruple Bottom Line: Corporate Governance and Sustainability in the 21st Century—a South African Perspective." Finance and Corporate Governance Conference Paper, November 22. Accessed July 15, 2016. https://ssrn.com/abstract=1713362. http://dx.doi.org/10.2139/ssrn.1713362.

Escobar, Arturo. 1995. *Encountering Development: The Making and Unmaking of the Third World*. Princeton, NJ: Princeton University Press.

Evans, R. Tripp. 2004. *Romancing the Maya: Mexican Antiquity in the American Imagination, 1820–1915*. Austin: University of Texas Press.

Fallaw, Ben. 2001. *Cárdenas Compromised: The Failure of Reform in Postrevolutionary Yucatán*. Durham, NC: Duke University Press. https://doi.org/10.1215/9780822380245.

Farrelly, Trisia Angela. 2011. "Indigenous and Democratic Decision-Making: Issues from Community-Based Ecotourism in the Bouma National Heritage Park, Fiji." *Journal of Sustainable Tourism* 19 (7): 817–35. https://doi.org/10.1080/09669582.2011.553390.

Farriss, Nancy Marguerite. 1984. *Maya Society under Colonial Rule: The Collective Enterprise of Survival*. Princeton, NJ: Princeton University Press.

Faust, Betty Bernice. 1998. *Mexican Rural Development and the Plumed Serpent: Technology and Maya Cosmology in the Tropical Forest of Campeche, Mexico*. Westport, CT: Bergin and Garvey.

Faust, Betty Bernice, Eugene Newton Anderson, and John G. Frazier. 2004. *Rights, Resources, Culture, and Conservation in the Land of the Maya*. New York: Greenwood.

Faux, Jeffrey. 2005. "Theoretical and Practical Contexts of Triple Bottom Line Performance and Reporting: Implications for the Tourism Sector." *Tourism Review International* 9 (1): 95–105. https://doi.org/10.3727/154427205774791753.

Ferguson, James, and Akhil Gupta. 2002. "Spatializing States: Toward an Ethnography of Neoliberal Governmentality." *American Ethnologist* 29 (4): 981–1002. https://doi.org/10.1525/ae.2002.29.4.981.

Fine, Ben. 2001. *Social Capital versus Social Theory: Political Economy and Social Science at the Turn of the Millennium*. New York: Routledge. https://doi.org/10.4324/9780203470787.

Fischer, Edward F. 1999. "Cultural Logic and Maya Identity." *Current Anthropology* 40 (4): 473–500.

Fischer, Edward F. 2001. *Cultural Logics and Global Economies: Maya Identity in Thought and Practice*, 1st ed. Austin: University of Texas Press.

Fischer, Michael, and George M. Marcus. 1986. *Anthropology as Cultural Critique: An Experimental Moment in the Human Sciences*. Chicago: University of Chicago Press.

Flora, Cornelia Butler. 1990. "Presidential Address: Rural Peoples in a Global Economy." *Rural Sociology* 55 (2): 157–77. https://doi.org/10.1111/j.1549-0831.1990.tb00678.x.

Foster, George M. 1943. "The Geographical, Linguistic, and Cultural Position of the Popoluca of Veracruz." *American Anthropologist* 45 (4): 531–46. https://doi.org/10.1525/aa.1943.45.4.02a00040.

Foster, George M. 1965. "Peasant Society and the Image of Limited Good." *American Anthropologist* 67 (2): 293–315. https://doi.org/10.1525/aa.1965.67.2.02a00010.

Foucault, Michel. 1991. *The Foucault Effect: Studies in Governmentality: With Two Lectures by and an Interview with Michel Foucault.* Ed. Graham Burchell, Colin Gordon, and Peter Miller. Chicago: University of Chicago Press.

Foucault, Michel. 2003. *The Birth of the Clinic: An Archaeology of Medical Perception.* London: Psychology Press.

Fox, John W., Marie Charlotte Arnauld, Wendy Ashmore, Marshall Joseph Becker, Gordon Brotherston, Lyle Campbell, William J. Folan, John S. Henderson, Nedenia C. Kennedy, Robert J. Sharer et al. 1981. "The Late Postclassic Eastern Frontier of Mesoamerica: Cultural Innovation along the Periphery [and Comments and Replies]." *Current Anthropology* 22 (4): 321–46. https://doi.org/10.1086/202685.

Friedlander, Judith. 2006. *Being Indian in Hueyapan: A Revised and Updated Edition,* 2nd ed. New York: Palgrave Macmillan. https://doi.org/10.1057/9780230601659.

Gabbert, Wolfgang. 2004. *Becoming Maya: Ethnicity and Social Inequality in Yucatán since 1500.* Tucson: University of Arizona Press.

García Canclini, Néstor. 1989. *Culturas híbridas: Estrategias para entrar y salir de la modernidad.* Mexico City: Grijalbo.

García Canclini, Néstor. 1993. *Transforming Modernity: Popular Culture in Mexico.* Austin: University of Texas Press.

García Canclini, Néstor. 1999. "Los Usos Sociales Del Patrimonio Cultural." *Patrimonio Etnológico, Nuevas Perspectivas de Estudio.* Accessed June 24, 2018. http://observatorio cultural.udgvirtual.udg.mx/repositorio/handle/123456789/130.

Garrett, William E. 1989. "La Ruta Maya." *National Geographic* 176 (4): 424–79.

Gasca Zamora, José, Gustavo López Pardo, Bertha Palomino Villavicencio, and Martín Mathus Alonso. 2010. *La gestión comunitaria de recursos naturales y ecoturísticos en la Sierra Norte de Oaxaca.* Mexico City, Distrito Federal: Universidad Nacional Autónoma de México, Instituto de Investigaciones Económicas. Accessed June 24, 2018. http://ru.iiec.unam.mx/27/.

Gaskins, Suzanne. 2003. "From Corn to Cash: Change and Continuity within Mayan Families." *Ethos* 31 (2): 248–73. https://doi.org/10.1525/eth.2003.31.2.248.

Gledhill, John. 2004. "Neoliberalism." In *A Companion to the Anthropology of Politics,* ed. David Nugent and Joan Vincent, 332–48. Hoboken, NJ: Wiley-Blackwell.

Goffman, Erving. 1999. *The Presentation of Self in Everyday Life.* New York: Doubleday.

Goldkind, Victor. 1965. "Social Stratification in the Peasant Community: Redfield's Chan Kom Reinterpreted." *American Anthropologist* 67 (4): 863–84. https://doi.org/10.1525/aa.1965.67.4.02a00010.

Goldring, Luin. 1996. "The Changing Configuration of Property Rights under Ejido Reform." In *Reforming Mexico's Agrarian Reform,* ed. Laura Randall, 271–87. New York: M. E. Sharpe.

Gonzales, Michael J. 2002. *The Mexican Revolution, 1910–1940.* Albuquerque: University of New Mexico Press.

Greenwood, Davydd J., William Foote Whyte, and Ira Harkavy. 1993. "Participatory Action Research as a Process and as a Goal." *Human Relations* 46 (2): 175–92. https://doi.org/10.1177/001872679304600203.

Gregory, James R., Peter J. Bertocci, Henri J.M. Claessen, Matthew Cooper, Peter Coy, Alain Y. Dessaint, Ronald J. Duncan, George M. Foster, Charles A. Lave, Grant McCall, Thomas J. Maloney, Manning Nash, Claude Robineau, Richard F. Salisbury, Harold K. Schneider, and Sharon W. Tiffany. 1975. "Image of Limited Good, or Expectation of Reciprocity? [and Comments and Reply]." *Current Anthropology* 16 (1): 73–92. https://doi.org/10.1086/201518.

Grootaert, Christiaan, and Thierry Van Bastelaer. 2002. *Understanding and Measuring Social Capital: A Multidisciplinary Tool for Practitioners*, vol. 1. Washington, DC: World Bank Publications. https://doi.org/10.1596/0-8213-5068-4.

Haenn, Nora. 2005. *Fields of Power, Forests of Discontent: Culture, Conservation, and the State in Mexico*. Tucson: University of Arizona Press.

Hall, C. Michael. 1999. "Rethinking Collaboration and Partnership: A Public Policy Perspective." *Journal of Sustainable Tourism* 7 (3–4): 274–89.

Hames, Raymond. 2007. "The Ecologically Noble Savage Debate." *Annual Review of Anthropology* 36 (1): 177–90. https://doi.org/10.1146/annurev.anthro.35.081705.123321.

Hannerz, Ulf. 1990. "Cosmopolitans and Locals in World Culture." *Nationalism, Globalization, and Modernity* 7 (2–3): 237–51.

Hanson, Craig A. 2008. "The Late Mesoamerican Village." PhD dissertation, Tulane University, New Orleans, LA.

Harvey, David B. 2000. "Cosmopolitanism and the Banality of Geographical Evils." *Public Culture* 12 (2): 529–64. https://doi.org/10.1215/08992363-12-2-529.

Hays-Mitchell, Maureen. 2002. "Resisting Austerity: A Gendered Perspective on Neo-Liberal Restructuring in Peru." *Gender and Development* 10 (3): 71–81. https://doi.org/10.1080/13552070215920.

Hendon, Julia A., and Rosemary A. Joyce. 2004. *Mesoamerican Archaeology: Theory and Practice*, vol. 1. Hoboken, NJ: Wiley-Blackwell.

Hervik, Peter. 1998. "The Mysterious Maya of National Geographic." *Journal of Latin American Anthropology* 4 (1): 166–97. https://doi.org/10.1525/jlca.1998.4.1.166.

Hervik, Peter. 1999. *Mayan People within and beyond Boundaries: Social Categories and Lived Identity in Yucatán*. Studies in Anthropology and History, vol. 25. Amsterdam: Harwood Academic Publishers.

Houck, Charles Weston. 2004. "Rural Survey of Ek Balam, Yucatan, Mexico." PhD dissertation, Tulane University, New Orleans, LA.

Hutson, Scott R., Galvin Can Herrera, and Gabriel Adrian Chi. 2014. "Maya Heritage: Entangled and Transformed." *International Journal of Heritage Studies* 20 (4): 376–92. https://doi.org/10.1080/13527258.2012.756422.

INEGI (Instituto Nacional de Estadística y Geografía). 2003. "Censo Ejidal 2001 Participación en PROCEDE—documentación obtenida—2001—entidad federativa."

Diciembre. Accessed June 24, 2018. http://internet.contenidos.inegi.org.mx
/contenidos/Productos/prod_serv/contenidos/espanol/bvinegi/productos/censos
/poblacion/poblacion_indigena/leng_indi/PHLI.pdf.

INEGI (Instituto Nacional de Estadística y Geografía). 2009. "Perfil sociodemográ-
fico de la población que habla lengua indígena." Mexico City: Instituto Nacional
de Estadística y Geografía. Accessed June 24, 2018. http://internet.contenidos.inegi
.org.mx/contenidos/Productos/prod_serv/contenidos/espanol/bvinegi/productos
/censos/poblacion/poblacion_indigena/leng_indi/PHLI.pdf.

INEGI (Instituto Nacional de Estadística y Geografía). 2010. "Censo de Población Y
Vivienda, 2010: Cuestionario Básico." Mexico City: Instituto Nacional de Estadística y
Geografía. Accessed June 24, 2018. http://www3.inegi.org.mx/sistemas/temas
/default.aspx?s=est&c=21702.

Jackson, Clark. 1997. "Sustainable Development at the Sharp End." *Development in Practice* 7 (3): 237–47. https://doi.org/10.1080/09614529754477.

Jafari, Jafar. 1987. "Tourism Models: The Sociocultural Aspects." *Tourism Management* 8
(2): 151–59. https://doi.org/10.1016/0261-5177(87)90023-9.

Jones, Samantha. 2005. "Community-Based Ecotourism: The Significance of Social Capital." *Annals of Tourism Research* 32 (2): 303–24. https://doi.org/10.1016/j.annals.2004
.06.007.

Joseph, Gilbert Michael, and Daniel Nugent. 1994. *Everyday Forms of State Formation:
Revolution and the Negotiation of Rule in Modern Mexico*. Durham, NC: Duke University Press.

Juárez, Ana M. 2002. "Ecological Degradation, Global Tourism, and Inequality: Maya
Interpretations of the Changing Environment in Quintana Roo, Mexico." *Human
Organization* 61 (2): 113–24. https://doi.org/10.17730/humo.61.2.dbyeyrdgccoc5kga.

Katz, Friedrich. 2014. *Riot, Rebellion, and Revolution: Rural Social Conflict in Mexico*.
Princeton, NJ: Princeton University Press.

Kintz, Ellen R. 1990. *Life under the Tropical Canopy: Tradition and Change among the Yucatec
Maya*. Austin, TX: Holt, Rinehart, and Winston.

Kintz, Ellen R. 1998. "The Yucatec Maya Frontier and Maya Women: Tenacity of Tradition and Tragedy of Transformation." *Sex Roles* 39 (7): 589–601. https://doi.org/10
.1023/A:1018843730762.

Kirchhoff, Paul. 1943. "Mesoamérica, Sus Límites Geográficos, Composición Étnica Y
Caracteres Culturales." *Acta Americana* 1: 92–107.

Kirshenblatt-Gimblett, Barbara. 1998. *Destination Culture: Tourism, Museums, and Heritage*.
Berkeley: University of California Press.

Klepeis, Peter, and Colin Vance. 2003. "Neoliberal Policy and Deforestation in South-
eastern Mexico: An Assessment of the PROCAMPO Program." *Economic Geography*
79 (3): 221–40. https://doi.org/10.1111/j.1944-8287.2003.tb00210.x.

Knorr-Cetina, Karin, and Rom Harré. 1981. *The Manufacture of Knowledge*. Oxford:
Pergamon.

Lange, Frederick W. 1976. "The Northern Central American Buffer: A Current Perspective." *Latin American Research Review* 11: 177–83.

Larson, Patricia, Mark S. Freudenberger, and Barbara Wyckoff-Baird. 1998. *WWF Integrated Conservation and Development Projects: Ten Lessons from the Field, 1985–1996*. Washington, DC: World Wildlife Fund.

Levy, Philip I. 1997. "A Political-Economic Analysis of Free-Trade Agreements." *American Economic Review* 87 (4): 506–19.

Lewis, Oscar. 1947. "Wealth Differences in a Mexican Village." *Scientific Monthly* 65: 127–32.

Lewis, Oscar. 1960. *Tepoztlán: Village in Mexico*. New York: Holt.

Lewis, Oscar. 1975. *Five Families: Mexican Case Studies in the Culture of Poverty*. New York: Basic Books.

Li, Wen Jun. 2006. "Community Decisionmaking Participation in Development." *Annals of Tourism Research* 33 (1): 132–43. https://doi.org/10.1016/j.annals.2005.07.003.

Little, Walter E. 2000. "Home as a Place of Exhibition and Performance: Mayan Household Transformations in Guatemala." *Ethnology* 39 (2): 163–81. https://doi.org/10.2307/3773842.

Little, Walter E. 2004a. "Performing Tourism: Maya Women's Strategies." *Signs* 29 (2): 528–33. https://doi.org/10.1086/378105.

Little, Walter E. 2004b. *Mayas in the Marketplace: Tourism, Globalization, and Cultural Identity*. Austin: University of Texas Press.

Littlefield, Alice. 1978. "Exploitation and the Expansion of Capitalism: The Case of the Hammock Industry of Yucatan." *American Ethnologist* 5 (3): 495–508. https://doi.org/10.1525/ae.1978.5.3.02a00050.

Loewe, Ronald. 2009. "Maya Reborn." *Revista de Antropologia* 38 (3): 237–62.

Loewe, Ronald. 2010. *Maya or Mestizo? Nationalism, Modernity, and Its Discontents*. Toronto: University of Toronto Press.

Loewe, Ronald, and Sarah Taylor. 2008. "Neoliberal Modernization at the Mexican Periphery: Gender, Generation, and the Construction of a New, Flexible Workforce." *Urban Anthropology and Studies of Cultural Systems and World Economic Development* 37 (3–4): 357–92.

Low, Setha M., Dana Taplin, and Suzanne Scheld. 2005. *Rethinking Urban Parks: Public Space and Cultural Diversity*. Austin: University of Texas Press.

MacCannell, Dean. 1976. *The Tourist: A New Theory of the Leisure Class*. Berkeley: University of California Press.

Magnoni, Aline, Traci Ardren, and Scott Hutson. 2007. "Tourism in the Mundo Maya: Inventions and (Mis)Representations of Maya Identities and Heritage." *Archaeologies* 3 (3): 353–83. https://doi.org/10.1007/s11759-007-9042-8.

Mallon, Florencia E. 1995. *Peasant and Nation: The Making of Postcolonial Mexico and Peru*. Berkeley: University of California Press.

Mansuri, Ghazala, and Vijayendra Rao. 2004. "Community-Based and -Driven Development: A Critical Review." *World Bank Research Observer* 19 (1): 1–39. https://doi.org/10.1093/wbro/lkho12.

Mansuri, Ghazala, and VijayendraRao. 2007. "Update Note on Community-Based and -Driven Development." Mimeo. Washington, DC: World Bank.

Mattiace, Shannan, and Rodrigo Llanes Salazar. 2015. "Reformas Multiculturales Para Los Mayas de Yucatán." *Estudios Sociológicos* 33 (99): 607–32.

McGehee, Nancy Gard, Whitney Knollenberg, and Amy Komorowski. 2015. "The Central Role of Leadership in Rural Tourism Development: A Theoretical Framework and Case Studies." *Journal of Sustainable Tourism* 23 (8–9): 1277–97. https://doi.org/10.1080/09669582.2015.1019514.

McTaggart, Robert. 1997. *Participatory Action Research: International Contexts and Consequences.* Albany: State University of New York Press.

Medina, Laurie K. 2003. "Commoditizing Culture: Tourism and Maya Identity." *Annals of Tourism Research* 30 (2): 353–68. https://doi.org/10.1016/S0160-7383(02)00099-3.

Mitchell, Robert E., and Donald G. Reid. 2001. "Community Integration: Island Tourism in Peru." *Annals of Tourism Research* 28 (1): 113–39. https://doi.org/10.1016/S0160-7383(00)00013-X.

Molina Solis, Juan Francisco. 1896. *Historia del Descubrimiento y Conquista de Yucatan con una Resena de la Historia Antigua de Esta Peninsula.* Merida, Yucatán, Mexico: Imprenta y Litografia R. Caballero. Accessed June 24, 2018. https://archive.org/stream/historiadeldescoosolgoog#page/n7/mode/2up.

Monaghan, John. 1999. *The Covenants with Earth and Rain: Exchange, Sacrifice, and Revelation in Mixtec Sociality,* vol. 219. Norman: University of Oklahoma Press.

Morán, Emilio F. 1990. *The Ecosystem Approach in Anthropology: From Concept to Practice.* Ann Arbor: University of Michigan Press.

Muñoz-Fernández, Carmen. 2015. "Sun, Sand, and . . . Sacred Pyramids: The Mayanization of Cancun's Tourist Imaginary." *Archeological Papers of the American Anthropological Association* 25 (1): 68–73. https://doi.org/10.1111/apaa.12048.

Nash, June C. 2001. *Mayan Visions: The Quest for Autonomy in an Age of Globalization.* London: Psychology Press.

Nash, June C., and Maria P. Fernandez-Kelly. 1983. *Women, Men, and the International Division of Labor.* Albany: State University of New York Press.

Noronha, Raymond. 1976. "Review of the Sociological Literature on Tourism." 68497. World Bank. Accessed June 24, 2018. http://documents.worldbank.org/curated/en/478941468168563049/pdf/684970WP00OFFIoiteratureoonoTourism.pdf.

Nuijten, Monique. 2003a. "Family Property and the Limits of Intervention: The Article 27 Reforms and the PROCEDE Programme in Mexico." *Development and Change* 34 (3): 475–97. https://doi.org/10.1111/1467-7660.00315.

Nuijten, Monique. 2003b. *Power, Community, and the State: The Political Anthropology of Organisation in Mexico.* London: Pluto.

Nutini, Hugo G. 1996. "Mesoamerican Community Organization: Preliminary Remarks." *Ethnology* 35 (2): 81–92. https://doi.org/10.2307/3774071.

Nutini, Hugo G., Peter Carrasco, and James M. Taggart. 2009. *Essays on Mexican Kinship*. Pittsburgh: University of Pittsburgh Press.

Nyanzi, Stella, Ousman Bah, Sulayman Joof, and Gijs Walraven. 2007. "Ethnography and PRA among Gambian Traditional Birth Attendants: A Methods Discussion." *Qualitative Research* 7 (3): 317–26. https://doi.org/10.1177/1468794107078512.

Okazaki, Etsuko. 2008. "A Community-Based Tourism Model: Its Conception and Use." *Journal of Sustainable Tourism* 16 (5): 511–29. https://doi.org/10.1080/09669580802159594.

Ooi, Natalie, Jennifer Laing, and Judith Mair. 2015. "Social Capital as a Heuristic Device to Explore Sociocultural Sustainability: A Case Study of Mountain Resort Tourism in the Community of Steamboat Springs, Colorado, USA." *Journal of Sustainable Tourism* 23 (3): 417–36. https://doi.org/10.1080/09669582.2014.957211.

Overmyer-Velázquez, Rebecca. 2007. "Indian, Nation, and State in Neoliberal Mexico." *Latin American and Caribbean Ethnic Studies* 2 (1): 29–49. https://doi.org/10.1080/17442220601167293.

Overmyer-Velázquez, Rebecca. 2011. *Folkloric Poverty: Neoliberal Multiculturalism in Mexico*. University Park: Pennsylvania State University Press.

Palomino Villavicencio, C. Bertha, and A. Gustavo López Pardo. 2007. "Programa Ecoturismo En Zonas Indigenas." Mexico City: Comisión Nacional para el Desarrollo de los Pueblos Indígenas. Accessed June 24, 2018. http://www.cdi.gob.mx/coneval/evaluacion_ecotourismo_2006.pdf.

Palomino Villavicencio, C. Bertha, and A. GustavoLópez Pardo. 2012. "Indigenous Ecotourism in Quintana Roo Mexico: Case Study of Kantemo." *Book of Proceedings*, Vol. 1: 990–98. International Conference on Tourism and Management Studies, Algarve, Portugal, 2011.

Perkins, Harvey C., and David C. Thorns. 2001. "Gazing or Performing?" *International Sociology* 16 (2): 185–204. https://doi.org/10.1177/0268580901016002004.

Perramond, Eric P. 2008. "The Rise, Fall, and Reconfiguration of the Mexican Ejido." *Geographical Review* 98 (3): 356–71. https://doi.org/10.1111/j.1931-0846.2008.tb00306.x.

Pi-Sunyer, Oriel, R. Brooke Thomas, and Magali Daltabuit. 2001. "Tourism on the Maya Periphery." In *Hosts and Guests Revisited: Tourism Issues of the 21st Century*, ed. Valene L. Smith and Michael Brent, 122–40. Putnam Valley, NY: Cognizant Communication Corp.

Pollock, Sheldon, Homi K. Bhabha, Carol A. Breckenridge, and Dipesh Chakrabarty. 2000. "Cosmopolitanisms." *Public Culture* 12 (3): 577–89. https://doi.org/10.1215/08992363-12-3-577.

Re Cruz, Alicia. 1996. *The Two Milpas of Chan Kom: Scenarios of a Maya Village Life*. Albany: State University of New York Press.

Re Cruz, Alicia. 2003. "Milpa as an Ideological Weapon: Tourism and Maya Migration to Cancún." *Ethnohistory* 50 (3): 489–502. https://doi.org/10.1215/00141801-50-3-489.

Redfield, Robert. 1932. "Maya Archaeology as the Mayas See It." *Sociologus* 6: 298–309.

Redfield, Robert. 1941. *The Folk Culture of Yucatan.* Chicago: University of Chicago Press.

Redfield, Robert. 1950. *A Village That Chose Progress: Chan Kom Revisited.* Chicago: University of Chicago Press.

Redfield, Robert, and Alfonso Villa Rojas. 1934. *Chan Kom, a Maya Village.* Chicago: University of Chicago Press.

Redford, Kent H. 1991. "The Ecologically Noble Savage." *Cultural Survival Quarterly,* January 31, 46–48.

Registro Agrario Nacional. 2015. "Padrón E Historial de Núcleos Agrarios." Accessed January 15, 2015. http://www.ran.gob.mx/index.php/sistemas-de-consulta/phina.

Reid, Donald G. 2003. *Tourism, Globalization, and Development: Responsible Tourism Planning.* London: Pluto.

Restall, Matthew. 1999. *Maya Conquistador.* Boston: Beacon.

Reyes-Foster, Beatriz. 2012. "Grieving for Mestizaje: Alternative Approaches to Maya Identity in Yucatan, Mexico." *Identities* 19 (6): 657–72. https://doi.org/10.1080/1070289X.2012.734766.

Rickly-Boyd, Jillian M. 2013. "Existential Authenticity: Place Matters." *Tourism Geographies* 15 (4): 680–86. https://doi.org/10.1080/14616688.2012.762691.

Rogers, Maureen, and Roberta Ryan. 2001. "The Triple Bottom Line for Sustainable Community Development." *Local Environment* 6 (3): 279–89. https://doi.org/10.1080/13549830120073275.

Rothstein, Frances. 2007. *Globalization in Rural Mexico: Three Decades of Change,* 1st ed. Austin: University of Texas Press.

Ruhanen, Lisa. 2013. "Local Government: Facilitator or Inhibitor of Sustainable Tourism Development?" *Journal of Sustainable Tourism* 21 (1): 80–98. https://doi.org/10.1080/09669582.2012.680463.

Saarinen, Jarkko. 2006. "Traditions of Sustainability in Tourism Studies." *Annals of Tourism Research* 33 (4): 1121–40. https://doi.org/10.1016/j.annals.2006.06.007.

Sachs, Carolyn E. 1996. *Gendered Fields: Rural Women, Agriculture, and Environment,* 1st ed. Boulder: Westview.

Safa, Helen I. 2002. "Women and Globalization: Lessons from the Dominican Republic." In *The Spaces of Neoliberalism: Land, Place, and Family in Latin America,* ed. Jacquelyn Chase, 141–58. Bloomfield, CT: Kumarian.

Saldívar, Emiko. 2011. "Everyday Practices of Indigenismo: An Ethnography of Anthropology and the State in Mexico." *Journal of Latin American and Caribbean Anthropology* 16 (1): 67–89. https://doi.org/10.1111/j.1935-4940.2011.01125.x.

Sandstrom, Alan R. 1991. *Corn Is Our Blood: Culture and Ethnic Identity in a Contemporary Aztec Indian Village,* 1st ed. Civilization of the American Indian Series, vol. 206. Norman: University of Oklahoma Press.

Scheyvens, Regina, and Matt Russell. 2012. "Tourism and Poverty Alleviation in Fiji: Comparing the Impacts of Small- and Large-Scale Tourism Enterprises." *Journal of Sustainable Tourism* 20 (3): 417–36. https://doi.org/10.1080/09669582.2011.629049.

Schüren, Ute. 2003. "Reconceptualizing the Post-Peasantry: Household Strategies in Mexican Ejidos." *Revista Europea de Estudios Latinoamericanos y del Caribe* 75: 47–63. https://doi.org/10.18352/erlacs.9693.

Scrimgeour, Frank, and Catherine Iremonger. 2004. *Maori Sustainable Economic Development in New Zealand: Indigenous Practices for the Quadruple Bottom Line*. Hamilton, New Zealand: University of Waikato Press.

SECTUR (Secretaria de Turismo de Mexico). 2012. "Programa Pueblos Mágicos." Secretaria de Turismo de Mexico. Accessed June 24, 2018. https://www.gob.mx/sectur/acciones-y-programas/programa-pueblos-magicos.

SECTUR (Secreteria de Turismo de Mexico). 2014. "Cuenta de Viajeros Internacionales." DataTUR: Analysis Integral del Turism. Accessed June 24, 2018. http://www.datatur.sectur.gob.mx/SitePages/VisitantesInternacionales.aspx.

SECTUR (Secretaria de Turismo de Mexico). 2015. "Boletín 286: Cancun Y La Riviera Maya Los Destinos Más Visitados Por El Turismo Internacional." Accessed June 24, 2018. http://www.sectur.gob.mx/sala-de-prensa/2014/12/31/boletin-286-cancun-y-la-riviera-maya-los-destinos-mas-visitados-por-el-turismo-internacional/.

SEDETUR (Secretaria de Turismo del Estado de Quintana Roo). 2013. "Indicadores Turisticos, Enero-Diciembre 2013." Secretaria de Turismo del Estado de Quintana Roo. Accessed June 24, 2018. http://sedetur.qroo.gob.mx/estadisticas/indicadores/2013/Indicadores%20Turisticos%20Diciembre%202013.pdf.

SEFOTUR (Secretaria de Fomento Turistico del Estado de Yucatan). 2014. "Informe mensual sobre resultados de la actividad turística en el estado de Yucatán." Secretaria de Fomento Turistico del Estado de Yucatan. Accessed June 24, 2018. http://sedetur.qroo.gob.mx/estadisticas/indicadores/Indicadores%20Turisticos%202013.pdf.

Sharer, Robert J., and Loa P. Traxler. 2006. *The Ancient Maya*. Stanford, CA: Stanford University Press.

Sharpley, Richard. 2000. "Tourism and Sustainable Development: Exploring the Theoretical Divide." *Journal of Sustainable Tourism* 8 (1): 1–19. https://doi.org/10.1080/09669580008667346.

Sharpley, Richard, and David J. Telfer. 2002. *Tourism and Development: Concepts and Issues*, vol. 5. Bristol, UK: Channel View Books.

Simms, Anja. 2007. *Tourism: Creating a Framework for a Vehicle for Economic Development in Underdeveloped Societies*. Providence, RI: Brown University Press.

Simpson, Eyler N. 1937. *The Ejido: Mexico's Way Out*. Chapel Hill: University of North Carolina Press.

Smith, Michael E., and Marilyn A. Masson. 2000. *The Ancient Civilizations of Mesoamerica: A Reader*. Hoboken, NJ: Wiley-Blackwell.

Smith, Valene L. 1989. *Hosts and Guests: The Anthropology of Tourism*, 2nd ed. Philadelphia: University of Pennsylvania Press. https://doi.org/10.9783/9780812208016.

Soloaga, Isidro, and Gabriel Lara. 2008. "Mexico." In *Distortions to Agricultural Incentives in Latin America*, ed. Kym Anderson and Alberto Valdes, 243–73. Washington, DC: World Bank Publications.

Stephen, Lynn. 1993. *Restructuring the Rural Family: Ejidatario, Ejidataria, and Official Views of Ejido Reform*. Storrs: University of Connecticut Press.

Stephens, John Lloyd. 1841. *Incidents of Travel in Central America, Chiapas, and Yucatan*. New York: Harper and Brothers. https://doi.org/10.5962/bhl.title.84376.

Stephens, John Lloyd. 1843. *Incidents of Travel in Yucatan*. 2 vols. New York: Harper and Brothers.

Stonich, Susan C. 2005. "Enhancing Community-Based Tourism Development and Conservation in the Western Caribbean." In *Tourism and Applied Anthropologists*, ed. Tim Wallace, 77–86. National Association of Practicing Anthropologists Bulletin. Hoboken, NJ: Blackwell. https://doi.org/10.1525/napa.2005.23.1.77.

Stronza, Amanda. 2001. "Anthropology of Tourism: Forging New Ground for Ecotourism and Other Alternatives." *Annual Review of Anthropology* 30 (1): 261–83. https://doi.org/10.1146/annurev.anthro.30.1.261.

Tansley, Aurthur George. 1935. "The Use and Abuse of Vegetational Concepts and Terms." *Ecology* 16 (3): 284–307. https://doi.org/10.2307/1930070.

Tax, Sol. 1937. "The Municipios of the Midwestern Highlands of Guatemala." *American Anthropologist* 39 (3): 423–44. https://doi.org/10.1525/aa.1937.39.3.02a00060.

Tax, Sol. 1957. "Changing Consumption in Indian Guatemala." *Economic Development and Cultural Change* 5 (2): 147–58. https://doi.org/10.1086/449729.

Tax, Sol. 1972. *Penny Capitalism: A Guatemalan Indian Economy*. London: Octagon Books.

Tax, Sol, and Robert Redfield. 1968. *Heritage of Conquest: The Ethnology of Middle America*. New York: Cooper Square.

Taylor, Sarah R. 2008. "Gracias a Los Gringos: Negotiating Tourism and Community Development." MA thesis, California State University, Long Beach.

Taylor, Sarah R. 2014. "Maya Cosmopolitans: Engaging Tactics and Strategies in the Performance of Tourism." *Identities* 21 (2): 219–32. https://doi.org/10.1080/1070289X.2013.878250.

Taylor, Sarah R. 2017. "Issues in Measuring Success in Community-Based Indigenous Tourism: Elites, Kin Groups, Social Capital, Gender Dynamics, and Income Flows." *Journal of Sustainable Tourism* 25 (3): 433–49.

Telfer, David J., and Geoffrey Wall. 1996. "Linkages between Tourism and Food Production." *Annals of Tourism Research* 23 (3): 635–53. https://doi.org/10.1016/0160-7383(95)00087-9.

Teriman, Suharto, Tan Yigitcanlar, and Severine Mayere. 2009. "Sustainable Urban Development: A Quadruple Bottom Line Assessment Framework." In *The Second Infrastructure Theme Postgraduate Conference: Conference Proceedings*, 228–38.

Queensland University of Technology, Faculty of Built Environment and Engineering. Accessed June 24, 2018. https://eprints.qut.edu.au/29546/.

Torres, Rebecca Maria, and Janet D. Momsen. 2005. "Gringolandia: The Construction of a New Tourist Space in Mexico." *Annals of the Association of American Geographers* 95 (2): 314–35. https://doi.org/10.1111/j.1467-8306.2005.00462.x.

Turner, Victor W. 1969. *The Ritual Process: Structure and Anti-Structure.* New Brunswick, NJ: Aldine Transaction.

Tyrrell, Timothy, Cody Morris Paris, and Vernon Biaett. 2012. "A Quantified Triple Bottom Line for Tourism: Experimental Results." *Journal of Travel Research* 20 (10): 1–15. https://doi.org/10.1177/0047287512465963.

UN World Tourism Organization. 2009. "UNWTO World Tourism Barometer" 7 (3). Accessed June 24, 2018. https://www.e-unwto.org/doi/pdf/10.18111/wtobarometer eng.2009.7.3.1.

UNESCO. 2015. "Pre-Hispanic City of Chichen-Itza." UNESCO World Heritage Centre. Accessed June 24, 2018. http://whc.unesco.org/en/list/483.

UNESCO. 2017. "World Heritage List." Accessed June 24, 2018. http://whc.unesco.org/en/list/.

Urry, John. 1990. *The Tourist Gaze.* Thousand Oaks, CA: Sage.

Vanclay, Frank. 2004. "Impact Assessment and the Triple Bottom Line: Competing Pathways to Sustainability?" *Sustainability and Social Science Round Table Proceedings,* December 12, University of Technology, Sydney, NSW, 27–39.

Van den Berghe, Pierre L. 1994. *The Quest for the Other: Ethnic Tourism in San Cristóbal, Mexico.* Seattle: University of Washington Press.

Van den Berghe, Pierre L. 1995. "Marketing Mayas: Ethnic Tourism Promotion in Mexico." *Annals of Tourism Research* 22 (3): 568–88. https://doi.org/10.1016/0160-7383(95)00006-R.

Vargas de la Peña, Leticia, V. CastilloBorges, and Alfonso Lacadena García-Gallo. 1998. "Textos Glíficos de Ek'Balam (Yucatan, Mexico): Hallazgos de Las Temporadas de 1996–1998." Paper presented at the Seventh Encuentro de Investigadores del Area Maya, November, Universidad Autonoma de Campeche, Mexico.

Vázquez Léon, Luis.2003. *El Leviatán Arqueológico: Antropología de Una Tradición Científica En México,* 2nd ed. Mexico City: Centro de Investigaciones y Estudios Superiores de Antropologia Social.

Velasco, Maria. 2016. "Between Power and Rationality: Tourism Governance, Tourism Policy, Tourism Public Management, and Tourism Planning." *PASOS: Revista de Turismo Y Patrimonio Cultural* 14 (3, Special Issue): 577–94.

Villarreal, Andrés. 2014. "Ethnic Identification and Its Consequences for Measuring Inequality in Mexico." *American Sociological Review* 79 (4): 775–806. https://doi.org/10.1177/0003122414541960.

Vogt, Evan Z. 1969. *Zinacantan: A Maya Community in the Highlands of Chiapas.* Cambridge, MA: Belknap. https://doi.org/10.4159/harvard.9780674436886.

Walker, Cameron Jean. 2009. *Heritage or Heresy: The Public Interpretation of Archaeology and Culture in the Maya Riviera*. Tuscaloosa: University of Alabama Press.

Warman, Arturo. 1988. "Los Campesinos En El Umbral de Un Nuevo Milenio." *Revista Mexicana de Sociologia* 50 (1): 3–12. https://doi.org/10.2307/3540501.

Warren, Kay B., and Jean Elizabeth Jackson. 2003. *Indigenous Movements, Self-Representation, and the State in Latin America*. Austin: University of Texas Press.

Wearing, Stephen, and Matthew McDonald. 2002. "The Development of Community-Based Tourism: Re-Thinking the Relationship between Tour Operators and Development Agents as Intermediaries in Rural and Isolated Area Communities." *Journal of Sustainable Tourism* 10 (3): 191–206. https://doi.org/10.1080/09669 580208667162.

Weaver, David. 2010. "Indigenous Tourism Stages and Their Implications for Sustainability." *Journal of Sustainable Tourism* 18 (1): 43–60. https://doi.org/10.1080/09669 580903072001.

Wells, Allen, and Gilbert M. Joseph. 1996. *Summer of Discontent, Seasons of Upheaval: Elite Politics and Rural Insurgency in Yucatán, 1876–1915*. Stanford, CA: Stanford University Press.

Whatmore, Sarah. 1993. "Sustainable Rural Geographies?" *Progress in Human Geography* 17 (4): 538–47. https://doi.org/10.1177/030913259301700408.

Wilk, Richard R. 1997. *Household Ecology: Economic Change and Domestic Life among the Kekchi Maya in Belize*. DeKalb: Northern Illinois University Press.

Wolf, Eric R. 1955. "Types of Latin American Peasantry: A Preliminary Discussion." *American Anthropologist* 57 (3): 452–71. https://doi.org/10.1525/aa.1955.57.3.02a00050.

Wolf, Eric R. 1957. "Closed Corporate Peasant Communities in Mesoamerica and Central Java." *Southwestern Journal of Anthropology* 13 (1): 1–18. https://doi.org/10.1086/soutjanth.13.1.3629154.

Zepeda Lecuona, Guillermo R. 2003. "Cuatro años de Procede: avances y desafíos en la definición de derechos agrarios en México." Government. July 9. Accessed June 24, 2018. http://www.pa.gob.mx/publica/pa070903.htm.

Hinch, Thomas, 56
hmeen, 105, 106–7
host, guest and, 12, 55
Hotel Eden, 15, 18, 33, 61, 65, 77, 78, 81, 94;
    closure of, 28; reopening, 29
Hotel Zone, 4
hotels, 102, 107, 118
households, xiii, 40–41, 63; outside world and,
    117; term, 40
huipiles, 102, 108, 119, 121
Hurricane Wilma, 59
hurricanes, 28, 48, 59, 113

ICDPs. *See* integrated conservation and devel-
    opment projects
IDB. *See* Inter-American Development Bank
identity, 5, 128, 130; hiding, 13; Maya, 5, 20, 47,
    108, 110; multiple, 20; national, 11, 53
Ignacio (Nacho), 15–16, 18, 30, 50, 63, 64–65, 66,
    82, 99, 100, 101, 108; Lucas and, 83; volun-
    teers/CBT project and, 114
INAH. *See* Instituto Nacional de Antropología
    e Historia
income: categories, 118–19, 119 (fig.); cultural,
    126; household, 93 (fig.); sources of, 92–93,
    93 (fig.)
INDEMAYA. *See* Instituto para el Desarrolla de
    la Cultura Maya del Estado de Yucatán
indigeneity, 25, 110, 125, 127; commodification
    of, 80; politics of, 19
indigenous people, 5, 7, 23, 84, 126, 127; develop-
    ment and, 3
INEGI. *See* Instituto Nacional de Estadistica y
    Geografia
INI. *See* Instituto Nacional Indigena
Instituto Nacional de Antropología e Historia
    (National Institute of Anthropology and
    History) (INAH), 5, 7, 11, 12, 128
Instituto Nacional de Estadistica y Geografia
    (National Institute of Statistics and Geogra-
    phy) (INEGI), 34
Instituto Nacional Indigena (National Indig-
    enist Institute) (INI), 54, 104
Instituto para el Desarrolla de la Cultura Maya
    del Estado de Yucatán (Institute for the
    Development of the Maya Culture of the
    Yucatán State) (INDEMAYA), 54
integrated conservation and development
    projects (ICDPs), 88
Inter-American Development Bank (IDB), 4,
    52
Izamal, xii, 122

Jackson, Clark, 96
Joan, 15, 18, 30, 75, 78, 81; on Ek'Balam, 60–61;
    Hotel Eden and, 29, 33, 61, 65
Joya de Cerén, 12
Justino, quote of, 90

Kaxil Kan, 78, 94
kin groups, 39, 41, 61, 63, 91, 95, 96; member-
    ship in, 40; obligations of, 40; patrilineal
    organization in, 40 (fig.)
kinship, 10, 27, 37; as organizational structure,
    36; patterns of, 41; as social structure, 23, 38
Kintz, Ellen R., xvi, 120
Kirchhoff, Paul, 51
knowledge, 20, 25, 97, 99–100, 103, 126, 130, 131;
    cultural, 57, 87; distribution of, 109; ecologi-
    cal, 24; local, 57, 96; social, 57

La Ruta Maya, maps of, 46
labor, 53, 131; non-agrarian, 117; reform, 67;
    wage, 5; women's share of, 117
land grants, 42, 67
land ownership, 4, 68
land reform, 3, 62, 63, 124, 126; revising, 70–76
land tenure, 3, 62, 63
land use, 10, 63
Larson, Patricia, 88
Late to Terminal Classic site, 43
Levi-Strauss, Claude, 22
Lewis, Oscar, 85
little community, 19, 80, 87; domination of,
    91–96
Little, Walter E., 101, 117, 119; tourism and, 23,
    102, 129–30
Littlefield, Alice, xii, 117
Loewe, Ronald, 20, 47
Lopez kin group, 91
Lopez Pat, Miguel, 39
Low, Setha M., 36–37
Lucio, don, 43, 73

MacCannell, Dean, 22, 23, 103
maize, 23, 81, 83, 108
Mansuri, Ghazala, 57, 91, 96
mapping, 26–27, 31–35
Maria, 106, 113, 114
Mathews, Jennifer P., 127
May, Celestina, 40
May, Concepción, 39, 40
May, Florentina, 39, 40
May kin group, 39, 39 (fig.), 95–96
May Tuz, don Claudio, 38, 39

Communities, Ecology and Production for Sustainable Development), 54
Pueblos Mágicos (Magic Villages), 122–23

quadruple bottom line (QBL), 121
Quintana Roo, 3, 4, 12, 116, 127
Quirigua, 12

Rafael, don, 26, 49, 105; concerns of, 75–76; quote of, 75, 76, 89, 106
Rao, Vijayendra, 57, 91, 96
Re Cruz, Alicia, 87, 117
Redfield, Robert, 20, 52–53, 84, 107, 129, 170; commerce and, 87; folk-urban continuum and, 7; little community and, 87; reinterpretation of, 94–95
reforestation, 124; maps of, 45
Reid, Donald G., 56
"Relación de Tiquibalon," 42
research, 19, 44; anthropological, 80; conceptualization/practice/implementation of, 57; ethnographic, 85; further, 129–32; tourism, 56
resources: cultural, 12; economic, 122; ecological, 12; environmental, 122; natural, 12, 88, 91; social, 122
rituals, 51; Mayan, 105, 106, 107
Rosa, 15, 16, 17, 18, 30, 50, 65, 66, 82, 98, 113, 114, 115
Rothstein, Frances, 117
Ruperto, don, 73; quote of, 68, 76, 77

Saarinen, Jarkko, 57
Sachs, Jeffrey D., 86
Salvador, 15, 18, 30, 49, 64, 65, 66; educational options for, 98; Eugenio and, 81; Federico and, 114
San Cosme, 117
Sandstrom, Alan R., 80, 126
Santa Rita, 15, 49
Scheld, Suzanne, 37
Secretaria de Desarrolla Social (Social Development Secretariat) (SEDESOL), 115
Secretaria de Turismo de Mexico (National Secretary of Tourism) (SECTUR), 11, 122
Secretaria de Turismo del Estado de Yucatán (SECATUR-Yucatán), 11, 101, 107
Sharpley, Richard, 56, 57
Simms, Anja, 56
Simonelli, Jean M., 57, 124
Simpson, Eyler N., 66
social capital, 60; bottom line and, 121–24; bridging versus bonding, 112, 122; cultural capital and, 121

social outcomes, 121, 126
social relations, 36, 60, 62; *ejidal* model of, 95; quantitative/qualitative nature of, 112
social structure, 24, 27, 41, 79, 95, 103; kin-based, 38
Spanish Colonial, xi
Stephens, John Lloyd, 52
Stonich, Susan C., 58
Stronza, Amanda, 55
sustainability, xiii, 23, 25, 58, 111, 116, 122, 129, 130, 131, 132; corporate responsibility for, 121; financial, 111; long-term, 121; power and, 128; tourism and, 56–57

Taplin, Dana, 37
Tax, Sol, 84, 85, 120
TBL. *See* triple bottom line
Temozón, 8, 14, 14–15, 30, 33–34, 39, 48, 63, 67, 81, 82, 92, 118, 120; *ejido* of, 68, 70, 71; map of, 31
Terminal Classic, 7, 124
Tiendas Comunitarias Diconsa (Diconsa Community Stores), 81
Tikal, 12
Tiquibalon, 42, 100
tourism, xii, xiii, 10, 78, 94, 109–10, 130–31; alternative, 6, 55–56, 111; archaeological, 125; benefits of, 91, 112, 129; border zones, 6, 129; community-based, 8, 16, 17, 19, 22–24, 27–30, 35, 45, 48, 54, 55, 56, 59, 60, 61, 63, 65, 80, 87–91, 92 (fig.), 98, 101, 104, 107, 111, 116, 121, 122, 123, 125, 128, 129; cultural, 6, 34, 54; development of, 3, 4, 11, 12, 13, 14, 19, 21, 24, 25, 34, 47, 51, 52, 53–58, 59–60, 61, 74, 76, 80, 104, 110, 111, 113, 120, 125, 126, 128, 130; impact of, 5–6, 61; income from, 93 (fig.); indigenous, 12, 51–53, 56, 111, 116, 121, 125, 130; literature on, 12, 23, 61; mass, 6, 23, 53; performing, xiii, 41, 59, 92, 97, 101, 102, 110; predominance of, 117–18; sustainable, 56–57, 111, 122, 129; tradition and, 23, 130; typologies of, 6, 55
tourism industry, 51, 53, 57, 58, 87, 110, 125, 126; challenges for, xiii; employment in, 116–17
tourists, xi, xii, 6, 10, 12, 13, 16, 52, 61, 101; farming, 86; performances for, 106; stream of, 119; volunteer, 22, 51, 128
tradition, 97; culture and, 122; eradication of, 126; modernity and, 129; tourism and, 23, 130
traditional ecological knowledge (TEK), 24
triple bottom line (TBL), 111, 121, 125
Tulum, xi, xii, 4
Turner, Victor W., 79